COUNSELLING
• IN ACTION •

Series editor: *Windy Dryden*

Counselling in Action is a series of books developed especially for counsellors and students of counselling which provides clear and explicit guidelines for counselling practice. A special feature of the series is the emphasis it places on the *process* of counselling.

Feminist Counselling in Action
Jocelyn Chaplin

Gestalt Counselling in Action
Petrūska Clarkson

Transcultural Counselling in Action
Patricia d'Ardenne and Aruna Mahtani

Key Issues for Counselling in Action
edited by Windy Dryden

Psychodynamic Counselling in Action
Michael Jacobs

Person-Centred Counselling in Action
Dave Mearns and Brian Thorne

Transactional Analysis Counselling in Action
Ian Stewart

Cognitive-Behavioural Counselling in Action
Peter Trower, Andrew Casey and Windy Dryden

KEY ISSUES FOR
COUNSELLING

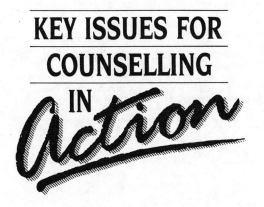

Edited by
WINDY DRYDEN

SAGE Publications
London • Newbury Park • New Delhi

Preface and Chapter 1 © Windy Dryden 1989

First published 1989

Chapter 2 is reprinted by kind permission of the American Association
for Counseling and Development from the *Personnel and Guidance
Journal* (1980), 59: 246–9.
Chapter 3 is reprinted by kind permission of the American Association
for Counseling and Development from the *Personnel and Guidance
Journal* (1983), 62: 163–6.
Chapter 4 is reprinted by kind permission of Hobsons Press Publishing
PLC from the *British Journal of Guidance and Counselling* (1982),
10(1): 44–50.
Chapter 5 is reprinted by kind permission of the British Association for
Counselling from *Counselling* (1987), 60: 14–20.
Chapter 6 is reprinted by kind permission of the American Association
for Counseling and Development from the *Personnel and Guidance
Journal* (1984), 62: 572–5.
Chapter 7 is reprinted by kind permission of Charles C. Thomas,
Publisher, from *The Social Influence Process in Counseling and
Psychotherapy* (1984) (ed. F. J. Dorn).
Chapter 8 is reprinted by kind permission of the American Association
for Counseling and Development from the *Personnel and Guidance
Journal* (1983), 62: 206–10.
Chapter 9 is reprinted by kind permission of the American Association
for Counseling and Development from the *Journal of Counseling and
Development* (1985), 63: 356–9.
Chapter 10 is reprinted by kind permission of the American Association
for Counseling and Development from the *Journal of Counseling and
Development* (1984), 63: 21–5.

 SAGE Publications Ltd
28 Banner Street
London EC1Y 8QE

SAGE Publications Inc
2111 West Hillcrest Drive
Newbury Park, California 91320

SAGE Publications India Pvt Ltd
32, M-Block Market
Greater Kailash – I
New Delhi 110 048

British Library Cataloguing in Publication data

Dryden, Windy
  Key issues for counselling in action. –
  (Counselling in action)
  1. Psychotherapy. Counselling
  I. Title II. Series
  616.89′14

ISBN 0-8039-8051-5
ISBN 0-8039-8052-3 Pbk

Library of Congress catalog card number 89-60327

Typeset by System 4 Associates Limited,
Farnham Common, Slough SL2 3PQ,
Printed in Great Britain by J. W. Arrowsmith Ltd, Bristol

Contents

To Pat Milner

Preface

A distinctive feature of the books in the *Counselling in Action* series is the emphasis placed on the developing counselling process. However, while most of the other books in the series have focused on specific approaches to counselling, the material in *Key Issues for Counselling in Action* reflects a variety of views on key issues that occur at different points in the counselling process. This diversity, in my view, will be more stimulating for readers than a single-authored text which, of necessity, would present a specific, but more limited viewpoint on these issues.

The book is structured as follows. In the introductory chapter I discuss one approach to understanding the therapeutic alliance in counselling as an integrating framework in which the material that follows in Chapters 2–10 can be placed. Then after each subsequent chapter, I present a number of discussion issues in the form of questions designed to encourage the reader to reflect personally on the material presented. My questions are only suggestive and readers are encouraged to develop their own. Readers might find it valuable to discuss their responses to both my and their own questions in a group context with colleagues or fellow students. Equally, the process of personal reflection on the issues raised can be done on one's own. However readers decide to use this book, it is my hope that it will serve both as a helpful text in encouraging deeper exploration of several key issues for counselling in action and as a useful adjunct to the other books in this series.

Windy Dryden
London

Acknowledgements

I wish to thank:

The American Association for Counseling and Development for granting permission for articles to be reprinted from the *Personnel and Guidance Journal* (Chapters 2, 3, 6, 8) and the *Journal of Counseling and Development* (Chapters 9, 10).

The British Association for Counselling for granting permission to reproduce Chapter 5 from their journal *Counselling*.

Hobsons Press for granting permission to reproduce Chapter 4 (in slightly modified form) from their journal the *British Journal of Guidance and Counselling*.

Charles C. Thomas for granting permission to reproduce Chapter 7 (in slightly modified form).

Finally, I wish to offer special thanks to all the contributors for agreeing so readily to be a part of this project.

Windy Dryden
London

1 The Therapeutic Alliance as an Integrating Framework

Windy Dryden

In this chapter I will briefly consider a perspective on the therapeutic alliance in counselling which, I hope, will serve as a framework in which the material presented in the rest of this book can be placed. The following chapters all focus on a key issue in counselling practice which deals with a different point in the counselling process. The view that asserts that counselling is a process which unfolds over time is, in my view, a crucial one. Counsellors are faced with different challenges at the beginning of counselling than they are during the middle and ending stages of this helping endeavour. Effective counsellors, then, in my opinion, are those who are flexible and skilful enough to modify their interventions according to the particular stage in which they and their clients are working. Effective counsellors also can vary their style of intervention according to the different needs of different clients.

The Therapeutic Alliance as an Integrating Framework

It is important to place the chapters that follow into a framework which views counselling from a broad perspective. I have chosen to outline briefly one such perspective which considers the work of counsellors to involve the initiation, maintenance and ending of the alliance that exists between them and their clients.

Bordin (1979) has written an important paper showing how the old psychoanalytic concept of the working alliance between counsellor and client (here referred to as the therapeutic alliance) can be broadened and divided into interrelated components. He argued that the therapeutic alliance — the interpersonal connectedness between counsellor and client — can be broken down into three such components: bonds, goals and tasks.

Bonds

When the *bond* between counsellor and client becomes a focus for consideration, certain counselling concepts are brought into view. The first, and perhaps the one that has received most attention in the literature,

concerns the interpersonal attitudes of the counsellor and their impact on the client. Such work has its roots in the person-centred tradition (Mearns and Thorne, 1988) but has a wider relevance. This work has shown that when the counsellor (a) demonstrates an empathic understanding of the client's concerns; (b) is genuine in the therapeutic encounter and (c) shows unconditional acceptance of the client as a person, and when the client experiences the presence of these counsellor-offered conditions, then the client tends to move to a position of greater psychological growth. Early arguments that such communicated (and perceived) counsellor attitudes were necessary and sufficient for client development have subsequently given way to the view that these attitudes are therapeutic under most but not all conditions. Indeed it is interesting to compare the views of Mearns and Thorne (1988) with those of Trower, Casey and Dryden (1988) on this point. For Mearns and Thorne such counsellor attitudes form the backbone of their book on person-centred counselling and the skilful communication of these attitudes constitutes the basic work of person-centred counsellors. For Trower, Casey and Dryden who write on cognitive-behavioural counselling, these attitudes are important in that they set the stage for the strategic and technical work that is to follow.

From a therapeutic alliance perspective, a more complex picture emerges that is in keeping with the present research position. On this issue see Beutler, Crago and Arizmendi, 1986. This position states that these counsellor attitudes are often important for most but not all clients. Here the task of the counsellor is to emphasise certain attitudes with some clients and to de-emphasise other attitudes with other clients in order to establish the most productive and idiosyncratic therapeutic bond with each individual client.

The second area that is relevant to our discussion of the therapeutic bond places more attention on the client's feelings and attitudes towards the counsellor. Here such concepts as the client's trust in the counsellor (see chapter 3), feelings of safety in the relationship, and degree of faith in the counsellor as a persuasive change agent become salient. While the focus of understanding how to best promote such client feelings and attitudes has been on constructive counsellor qualities and interventions, it is becoming increasingly recognised that clients bring with them to the counselling endeavour pre-formed tendencies in these areas which have a powerful impact on the counselling process (Moras and Strupp, 1982). Thus it may be that when a client has little trust in other people, finds them threatening to be with and has little or no faith in counselling as a vehicle for personal change then the phenomenon of 'client reluctance' is encountered (see Chapter 4). This is particularly so when, in addition, the client has, in some way, been coerced into seeking counselling 'help'.

The third area relevant to the therapeutic bond concerns work that has been done on the interpersonal styles of both client and counsellor. Here the focus is more interactive than in the previous two areas. The line of reasoning that has emerged from such work is that the counselling bond can be enhanced when the 'fit' between the interpersonal styles of counsellor and client is good and threatened when such a fit is poor. An example of a productive fit between counsellor and client, at least in the early stages of the relationship would be when the counsellor's style is 'dominant–friendly' and the client's style is 'submissive–friendly'. An example of an unproductive fit would be when the counsellor's style is 'passive–neutral' and the client's, 'submissive–hostile'. The implications from such work are that the counsellor's initial task is to modify his or her interpersonal style to complement the client's style in order to initiate the therapeutic alliance. Once such an alliance has been firmly established, the counsellor can begin to consider ways of slowly changing his or her style in the service of initiating client change. The important point here is that initial bonds which may be counter-therapeutic in the longer-term for client development may have to be established to get the relationship off the ground. This theme is the focus of Chapter 7 by Tracey.

Another implication of this work is that clients who have a critical/hostile style of interaction are more difficult to engage in counselling at the outset than clients who are appreciative/friendly. While the danger here is that clients who are critical and hostile get blamed for prematurely dropping out of counselling, the real implications of such a viewpoint concern alerting counsellors to very early signs of threat to the development of a productive alliance and encouraging them to focus on this in as constructive a way as possible. Indeed it has been shown that ignoring such threats does little to promote a constructive counselling relationship (Foreman and Marmar, 1985).

Another slightly different way of looking at the counsellor–client interactive bond has emerged from social psychology (Dorn, 1984). Here the focus has been on clients' expectations for counsellor participation and counsellors' use of a power base particularly in the early stage of counselling.

When clients show a preference for counsellor formality and demonstrations of expertise, then counsellors who seek to meet such expectations at least initially are more successful at initiating a productive therapeutic alliance than counsellors who try to encourage the clients to work in a relationship characterised by counsellor informality and friendliness. Clients who have such expectations seem to benefit more at the outset when counsellors use a power base consonant with these expectations. In this case, this means emphasising one's credibility as an expert and using a formal style of interaction. However, using such a power base may well have an impeding effect on clients who expect their counsellor to be more informal in style and to emphasise personal rather than professional qualities. With such clients, counsellors need to emphasise a power base characterised by informality, attractiveness and trustworthiness.

The point here is that counsellors who can appropriately vary their style of interaction and the power base in which such styles are rooted, are more likely to be more successful at initiating a therapeutic alliance than counsellors who use only one style of interaction and a single power base and expect their clients to adjust accordingly. The theme of counsellor variation is taken up in a slightly different way by Hutchins in Chapter 6 where counsellor variation is predicated upon client preferences for thinking, feeling and acting as dominant ways of dealing with the world.

The final area which is relevant to the bond between counsellor and client relates to the concepts of transference and counter-transference. Although these concepts have been derived from psychoanalytic approaches to counselling and psychotherapy (see Jacobs, 1988) and their very mention has a negative effect on many non-analytically-oriented counsellors, my position is that it is the phenomena to which the terms point that are more crucial than the use of terms themselves. The terms point to the fact that both clients and counsellors bring to the counselling relationship tendencies to perceive, feel and act towards another person which are influenced by their prior interaction with significant others. These tendencies can and often do have a profound influence on the development and maintenance of the therapeutic alliance.

Watkins (see Chapters 8 and 9) has aptly summarised the major ways in which such tendencies become manifest in the counselling relationship, and whichever terms one uses to describe such phenomena, the phenomena require understanding and constructive handling on the part of the counsellor.

Taking a process view of counselling with respect to bonds, the chapters by Fong and Cox (Chapter 3) and Manthei and Matthews (Chapter 4) have most relevance to the early stage of counselling; the chapters by Hutchins (Chapter 6) and Watkins (Chapters 8 and 9) span the early to middle stages, while the chapter by Tracey (Chapter 7) considers the concept of mutual influence in the therapeutic bond throughout the entire counselling process. Finally material pertaining to ending the therapeutic bond is dealt with in Chapter 10 by Ward.

It should not be forgotten that the development, maintenance and ending of the therapeutic bond (as with the other components of the therapeutic alliance to be considered) are influenced by the gender and racial composition of the counsellor–client pairing and I refer the reader to other books in this series for a full discussion of these issues (Chaplin, 1988; d'Ardenne and Mahtani, 1989).

Bordin's (1979) point about the importance of bonds in the therapeutic alliance is that the effectiveness of counselling and psychotherapy depends, to a large extent, on the development and maintenance of a productive bond between counsellor and client. I would like to stress here, as I have done earlier, that while the distinguishing feature of the bond in its early stages is one where there is a comfortable fit between counsellor and client, productive change is more often predicated upon the resolution of manageable conflict in the bond than it is on the perpetuation of early feelings of comfort in that relationship. Although it has to be said that some clients do benefit considerably from counselling relationships which are characterised by an enduring sense of comfort. Yet in most counselling relationships the counsellor needs to introduce dissonant elements (challenges) into the relationship so that the client can be encouraged to make changes in his or her style or acting, feeling and thinking.

Such dissonant elements or challenges, when constructive, need to be introduced in the context of a relationship based on solid foundations, that is, solid enough to survive the challenges thus introduced. The challenge may indeed be introduced by the client and Bordin makes the important point that from wherever the challenge originates the therapeutic alliance may indeed be strengthened by the successful resolution of a threat to its existence. It is where such a solid foundation in the relationship is absent that challenges have the greatest potential for therapeutic harm for the client (and in some instances, the counsellor). This issue of challenge and the resolution of conflict that it engenders is prevalent in a number of chapters in the book, in particular those by Fong and Cox (Chapter 3), Tracey (Chapter 7) and Watkins (Chapters 8 and 9).

Goals

The second component of the therapeutic alliance — goals — pertains to the objectives both client and counsellor have for coming together in the alliance. Goals are therefore the raison d'être of the counselling process. At first the issue of goals in the therapeutic alliance may seem deceptively simple; the client is in some kind of psychological distress, wants relief from this distress and wishes to live a more fulfilling life. The counsellor's goal is to help the client achieve his or her goals. However, the situation is often more complex than this and there are a number of issues that need to be discussed when goals become centre stage for consideration in the therapeutic alliance.

Before considering these issues, let us consider Bordin's (1979) major point about goals and use this as a starting point for considering the complexity of the subject. Bordin has argued that a good therapeutic outcome is facilitated when the counsellor and client agree what the client's goals are, and agree to work toward the fulfillment of these goals. Thus Bordin is concerned basically with outcome goals — that is, goals which are set as a criterion for the success, potential success, or failure of the counselling encounter at its end.

Whether such agreement over clients' goals should be explicit or implicit is a theme taken up by Sutton (Chapter 5) who is quite clear that goals should be explicitly set after the therapeutic bond has been initiated and after a period of initial assessment has been concluded.

Bordin's point alerts us to potential sources of failure and/or obstacles to the development of the counselling process. Thus the therapeutic alliance is threatened when either explicitly, or perhaps more commonly implicitly, the counsellor and client have different outcome goals in mind for the client.

This may occur for a variety of reasons. It often stems from prior disagreement, again often covert, concerning either how counsellor and client define the latter's problem or how the two account for the existence of the problem and how it is being maintained. An example of disagreement concerning problem definition is when the client considers that she has an anxiety problem whereas the counsellor considers that the client's problem is basically one of depression. As a result the alliance is threatened because when the client wishes to focus on her anxiety the counsellor wishes to focus on her presumed depression.

How can the counsellor and client deal with such a threat to the alliance? Obviously the first way is for the counsellor to realise that the threat exists and to assess correctly the source of that threat. But even then, and this is a point which I wish to underscore, there has to be some mechanism for the threat to be discussed. Of course the counsellor can make an adjustment in his view of the client's goals on the basis of a correct assessment without this being discussed. But here I wish to focus on the ensuing discussion between client and counsellor.

A productive feature of counselling exists, in my opinion, when client and counsellor can step back from the work that is being done and reflect together on the nature and effects of this work. If one thinks of both counsellor and client as having an experiencing part of themselves and an observing part (which can stand back and reflect on what has been experienced) then this process of reflection (called henceforth the reflection process) involves both client and counsellor stepping back and using the observing parts of themselves to reflect or what has gone before.

Coming back to our example, the counsellor and client can reflect (during the reflection process) on the counselling process and can begin to search for the source(s) of this threat to the alliance. If they both recognise that they differ concerning the nature of the client's basic problem, they can begin to talk about this and renegotiate a common as opposed to a disparate view of the problem. Without such a reflection process being part of the counselling relationship, the possibilities for reducing conflict occasioned by such differing viewpoints are reduced. Indeed, the establishment and maintenance of this reflection process means that counsellor and client have a forum for dealing with potential threats to the alliance in all three of its domains — bonds, goals and tasks.

Returning to our theme, if the counsellor and client agree (or come to agree) on a common definition of the client's problem they may still have differing views concerning how to account for this problem and its maintenance. It is here that counsellors are particularly influenced by their dominant theoretical orientation to counselling. Thus a cognitive-behavioural counsellor may have a very different view of the client's problem (see Trower, Casey and Dryden, 1988) from for example, a psychodynamically-orientated counsellor (see Jacobs, 1988). The important issue, from an alliance perspective, is not the inherent validity of one view over another; rather it is whether or not the counsellor and client share a common conceptualisation of the client's problem which will enable the work to proceed.

Referring the issue for discussion to the reflection process is again advocated here. The outcome of such discussion may be for the relationship to proceed because (a) the client has adjusted to or is prepared, for a while, to work on the basis of the counsellor's view; (b) the counsellor has adjusted to the client's view (it is interesting here to speculate how often counsellors do this); or (c) the client and counsellor have negotiated a new shared conceptualisation of the client's problem which is different from their previous initial attempts at understanding (this is an important but poorly understood topic awaiting future empirical enquiry). If the counsellor and client cannot come to some sort of shared understanding on this issue, the counsellor may, at this point, refer the client to a counsellor who will offer a conceptualisation of the client's problem more acceptable to the client.

While the client and counsellor now agree on problem definition and conceptualisation, they may still disagree concerning what to do about the problem. Thus a client and counsellor may agree that the client's problem is depression and have a shared conceptualisation of it but may disagree concerning what is to be done about the problem. The client may wish, for example, to minimise or reduce his depression whereas the counsellor may deem it productive for the client to tolerate his depression and not try to reduce it but to use it as an impetus for greater self-understanding.

This latter scenario points to a phenomenon quite common according to Maluccio (1979) in whose study counsellors were more ambitious concerning the kinds of changes they wanted their clients to achieve than were the clients themselves. Maluccio found that when clients in his study terminated counselling they were happier with what they had achieved from counselling than were their counsellors. The latter were dissatisfied that their clients had not achieved a fair measure of personality change, whereas the former were pleased with the changes in symptoms that they had achieved through counselling.

Extrapolating from this research it may be that while many clients seek goals which are relatively short-term in nature counsellors may see the transient quality of such changes and thus prefer to take a longer-term goals perspective and set goals which help to prevent future client relapse. In any event this is an issue that can again be referred for discussion to the reflection process.

While the emphasis so far has been on client outcome goals, other goals exist during counselling that require discussion. One set of goals are client goals that mediate the achievement of outcome goals (mediating goals). These may refer to changes that the client may exhibit outside the counselling process (external) or inside the process (internal). An example of a mediating external client goal might be for the client to successfully execute certain social skills in real life encounters, the achievement of which may help the client initiate friendships (outcome goal). An example of a mediating internal client goal might be for the client to successfully express feelings of annoyance towards the counsellor which may help the client confront his spouse (outcome goal). In addition to what has been said concerning shared agreement between counsellor and client concerning the latter's outcome goals (a point which also applies to the client's mediating goals), it is important that the client understands the therapeutic relevance of the relationship between the achievement of mediating goals and her outcome goals and commits herself to the achievement of these mediating goals. Without such understanding and commitment, the client may begin to feel that she is being asked to pursue goals that are meaningless to her. In which case referring the matter to the reflection process is once again advocated.

Another set of goals that needs to be considered here concerns the goals that the counsellor sets for him or herself during the counselling process. This is very frequently related to the goals the counsellor sets for the client. For example, if the counsellor believes it is important for the client to trust her, she may set for herself the goal of being especially accepting of the client's ambivalent feelings. Whereas at a later stage and given sufficient trust, she may endeavour to confront the attitudes that underpin such ambivalence. Thus, the goals that counsellors set for themselves are (or should be) heavily dependent upon their view of the client's position in the change process and effective counsellors are highly responsive to such considerations. This issue is explored in Chapter 6 by Hutchins who encourages counsellors to set goals for their own style of intervention while being mindful of the client's predominant style of dealing with the world.

While I am aware that some readers may object that this represents an overly mechanistic view of counselling and that effective counselling is often a highly intuitive activity, I would like to make the point in reply that intuition refers to sensitive judgments that have become internalised and appear, in highly skilled and experienced hands, effortless. However, at some point, these judgments were made at a conscious level and may even with experienced counsellors become conscious again when threats to the alliance appear.

Before leaving the topic of goals I would like to briefly list several points that need to be borne in mind when exploring goals with clients.

1 Clients may express goals in vague terms. Here it is important to help them specify them in a form that makes the goals achievable and, as Sutton argues in Chapter 5, subject to evaluation.

2 Clients may express goals that involve changes in other people or life events (for example, 'I want my mother to change', 'My goal is to have the local council find me better accommodation'). In individual counselling it is important to renegotiate goals so that their achievement falls within the client's power (for example, what is the client going to do differently to encourage her mother to change? What is the client going to do to persuade the council to find her better accommodation?).

3 Clients may express goals that are based on their disturbed feelings, attitudes or behaviour (for example, an anorexic client who wishes to lose more weight). Here it is important to deal with the level of disturbance first before setting concrete goals. It is for this reason that some counsellors prefer not to set goals too early in the counselling process.

4 Clients' goals change during the counselling process and thus counsellors need to update themselves on the current status of their clients' goals during the reflection process. (Some counsellors do this formally in specific review sessions.)

Tasks

The final component in this tripartite view of the therapeutic alliance pertains to tasks — activities carried out by both counsellor and client which are goal-directed in nature. Several books in this series have presented specific approaches to counselling in action where a predominant feature of each approach is its specification of the tasks that both counsellor and client are required to carry out in the service of meeting clients' goals (psychodynamic — Jacobs, 1988; person-centred — Mearns and Thorne, 1988; cognitive-behavioural — Trower, Casey and Dryden, 1988; Gestalt — Clarkson, 1989; and TA — Stewart, 1989). Such tasks may be broad in nature (for example, engage in the broad task of self-exploration in person-centred counselling) or more specific (engage in a two-chair dialogue in Gestalt counselling).

However, when an alliance perspective on tasks is taken, the slant is different from one which emphasises the content of such tasks and several questions become salient.

1.   Does the client understand the nature of the therapeutic tasks that she is being called upon to execute? If the client does not either explicitly or implicitly understand (a) that she has tasks to perform in the counselling process and (b) what these tasks are, then a potential obstacle to the client's progress through the counselling process appears. As with other potential obstacles this may be dealt with by referring the matter for discussion to that part of the counselling dialogue that I have termed 'the reflection process' where counsellor and client step back and discuss what has gone on between them during counselling sessions.

Aware of how important it is for clients to understand their role in the counselling process and more specifically what their tasks are in that process, some counsellors formally attempt to initiate clients into their role at the outset. This topic and the issues which it raises is discussed in Chapter 2 by Day and Sparacio.

2.   If the client understands the nature of the tasks that she is called upon to execute, does she see the instrumental value of carrying out these tasks? As noted earlier tasks are best conceptualised as ways of achieving therapeutic goals. Thus a client may understand what her tasks are but may be uncertain how carrying these out may help her to achieve her outcome goals. For example, a client may wish to handle interpersonal conflict in a more constructive way, for example by being assertive with his spouse rather than aggressive. However he may not see the link between being able to do this and being asked to free associate in the relatively unstructured setting of psychodynamic counselling. Alternatively another client may not see how disputing her irrational beliefs about competence (as required in cognitive-behavioural counselling) will necessarily help her to overcome her examination anxiety. Thus, from an alliance perspective it is very important that clients be helped to understand the link between carrying out their counselling tasks and achieving their outcome goals. This holds true whether the client's tasks are to be performed within the counselling session or between counselling sessions in their everyday lives.

3.   Does the client have the ability to carry out the therapeutic tasks required of her? The question of ability is important since although the execution of particular tasks may facilitate client change, if the client is unable to carry out these then this poses a threat to the therapeutic alliance. It may be productive, therefore, for clients to receive specific training in executing their tasks if they are unable to do so at a given point. For example, the client task of disputing irrational beliefs in cognitive-behavioural counselling involves the following client sub-tasks: (a) becoming aware of feeling emotionally distressed; (b) identifying one or more irrational beliefs that underpin such distress; (c) questioning the irrationality implicit in such beliefs; (d) answering one's questions in a persuasive way; and (e) replacing one's irrational beliefs with more rational alternatives. It is hopefully clear from such a detailed analysis of client task behaviour that the client's ability to successfully execute such a task depends upon (a) how effective the counsellor has been in training the client to do this within the counselling sessions and (b) how much successful practice the client has undertaken both within and between sessions.

It may be the case, however, that a client's lack of personal resources, whether intellectual in nature or attributable to current levels of emotional disturbance, may impede the client's ability to perform a given task. In such cases it is the counsellor's responsibility to modify the task accordingly or ensure that the client is able to carry out a different task more suited to the client's *present* level of ability.

4. *Does the client have the confidence to execute the task?* A similar point can be made here as has been made above. Certain client tasks (and in particular those that clients are asked to execute between sessions — the so-called 'homework assignments') require a certain degree of task confidence on the part of the client if she is to execute it successfully. So the client may understand the nature of the task, see its therapeutic relevance, have the ability to carry it out but may not do so because she predicts that she doesn't have the confidence to do it. Here the counsellor is called upon to help prepare the client in one of two ways. First, the counsellor may need to help the client practise the task in controlled conditions (usually within the counselling session) to the extent that she feels confident to do it on her own. Secondly, the counsellor may encourage the client to carry out the task unconfidently, pointing out that confidence comes from the result of undertaking an activity (that is, from practice) and is rarely experienced before the activity is first attempted. Counsellors who use analogies within the experience of the client (for example, learning to drive a car) often succeed at helping the client understand this important point.

5. *Does the task have sufficient therapeutic potency to facilitate goal achievement?* If all the aforementioned conditions (that is, the client understands the nature and therapeutic relevance of task execution, and she has sufficient ability and confidence to perform the task) are met, the client may still not gain therapeutic benefit from undertaking a task because the task does not have sufficient therapeutic potency to help the client achieve her goals. For example, certain client tasks, if sufficiently well carried out, will probably lend to client change. Thus exposing oneself, *in vivo* or through imagination, to a phobic object will likely yield some therapeutic benefit (Rachman and Wilson, 1980). However, certain tasks may have much less therapeutic potency to achieve a similar result. Thus it has yet to be demonstrated that free association or disputing one's irrational beliefs (in the counselling session rather than in the feared situation) has much therapeutic effect in overcoming phobias. Here then the counsellor's task is to become *au fait* with the current research literature on the subject at hand and not discourage the client by encouraging her to carry out a task which is unlikely, even under

the most favourable conditions, to produce much therapeutic benefit.

In this respect there are certain client problems which do seem to call for the execution of specific client tasks. Apart from phobic problems mentioned above, obsessive–compulsive problems seem to call for the client to employ some variant of response prevention in their everyday lives (Rachman and Wilson, 1980) and problems of depression seem to call for the client to modify distorted thought patterns (Beck et al., 1979) and troublesome elements of their significant interpersonal relationships (Klerman et al., 1984) in order to gain therapeutic benefit. It must be stressed, however, that our current knowledge does not yield detailed therapeutic task-related menus for a wide range of specific client problems and for the most part performing a wide variety of tasks may yield a comparable therapeutic result (Stiles, Shapiro and Elliott, 1986). In which case the issues detailed above (points 1–4) become particularly salient.

6. *Does the client understand the nature of the counsellor's tasks and how these relate to her own?* So far I have focused on issues which deal with clients' tasks. However, in addition to the foregoing, it is important that the client understands (either at an explicit or implicit level) the counsellor's interventions and their rationale. In particular the more the client can understand how her tasks relate to the tasks of her counsellor, the more each can concentrate on effective task execution, the purpose of which, as has been stressed above, is to facilitate the attainment of the client's goals. Should the client be puzzled concerning the counsellor's tasks and how these relate to her own she will be sidetracked from performing her own tasks and begin to question what the counsellor is doing and perhaps even the counsellor's competence. These doubts, if not explored and dealt with in the reflection process, constitute a threat at all levels of the therapeutic alliance. An additional strategy that may prevent the development of client's doubts is for the counsellor to explain at an appropriate stage in the counselling process, his tasks and why he is intervening in the way he has chosen to do. This is akin to the use of structuring discussed by Day and Sparacio in Chapter 2 and can be usefully linked to a discussion of the client's complementary tasks.

Counsellor Skill

Until quite recently the issue of counsellors' skill in executing their tasks in the therapeutic process has received little attention in the counselling literature. However recent investigations (for example, Luborsky et al., 1985) have brought to light an important and quite obvious point that the skill in which counsellors perform their own tasks in therapy has a positive influence on client outcome. From an alliance perspective, the degree to which clients make progress may be due in some measure to the skill with which counsellors perform their tasks. This means that we must not assume that even well trained counsellors demonstrate equal skill in performing their tasks. A further implication is that skill factors need more prominent attention in counsellor training and supervision than has hitherto been the case. Trainers and supervisors require concrete and detailed evidence concerning how skilfully counsellors have executed their tasks and need to rely less upon counsellors' descriptions of what they did in counselling sessions and more on specific ways of appraising skill (for example, through audio-taped cassette recordings of counselling sessions or at the very least through very detailed process notes).

Varying the Use of Counsellors' Tasks
A theme that has run through this chapter so far, albeit implicitly, is that since clients vary (along several key dimensions), counsellors need to vary accordingly their own contribution to the counselling process. This point is well made by Hutchins (Chapter 6) who argues that counsellors can improve the relationship they have with their clients by varying the tasks they use with different clients. While he focuses on the client's predominant modes of dealing with the world, he makes the point that counsellors too have similar predominant modes. While in an ideal world, effective counsellors would, with equal facility, be able to use cognitive, behavioural and affective tasks, the fact that counsellors have their own limitations means that it is a temptation for counsellors to restrict themselves to using tasks which reflect their predominant orientation (cognitive, emotive or behavioural). Hutchins's analysis implies that should counsellors restrict themselves to using particular intervention modes (that is, cognitive, emotive or behavioural), they would help a smaller range of clients than they could help if they became more flexible in freely and appropriately using cognitive, emotive and behavioural tasks. It follows from this that to increase their effectiveness in the task domain of the alliance, counsellors need to acknowledge their own task preferences *and* work on broadening their own range of task behaviour — a task which itself calls for continual exposure to what therapeutic models other than their own preferred model have to offer. This would mean that counsellors of different orientations would learn from each other to a greater extent than is currently the case, a point which would hasten the move towards eclecticism and integration in counselling and psychotherapy, now gathering momentum on both sides of the Atlantic.

The Three Components of the Therapeutic Alliance are Interrelated

So far I have dealt with the three components of the therapeutic alliance — bonds, goals and tasks — as if they were separate. In reality, however, they are interrelated, and I will bring this introductory chapter to a close by focusing on a few ways in which they do interrelate. In exemplifying this point, I will draw upon the material to be presented in the following chapters.

1   Successful structuring of the counsellor and client task behaviour in the counselling process (Day and Sparacio, Chapter 2) can help to strengthen the initial bond between counsellor and client and serve to clarify the client's goals (Sutton, Chapter 5).

2   Skilful responding to a client's early test of trust in the counselling relationship (Fong and Cox, Chapter 3) can free the client to engage more deeply in the counselling process (that is, it will deepen the bond between counsellor and client and enable the client to concentrate on his/her own task behaviour).

3   Sensitive and effective handling of client reluctance (Manthei and Matthews, Chapter 4) will increase the likelihood that the 'reluctant' client will commit himself to the counselling process and set goals that are relevant to himself (rather than to any coercive third party).

4   Specifying and agreeing a client's goals helps to ensure that both counsellor and client are working to the same end, facilitates a working bond and enables client and counsellor to choose more appropriate tasks to achieve the agreed and specified goals (Sutton, Chapter 5).

5   Selecting tasks that meet a client's predominant pattern of dealing with the world (Hutchins, Chapter 6) encourages the counsellor to speak the client's 'language' and serves to strengthen the therapeutic bond by helping the client feel understood in the task domain of the alliance.

6   Meeting a client's expectations for counselling early in the relationship helps to establish a solid relationship (bond) into which appropriate challenges (tasks) can be introduced in the middle stages of the work to facilitate client change (Tracey, Chapter 7).

7   Becoming aware and handling sensitively so-called transference phenomena (Watkins, Chapters 8 and 9) militates against the development of self- and relationship-defeating patterns in the counselling process and helps clients achieve their goals more effectively.

8   Skilful handling of the termination process and the client's attempts to terminate a counselling relationship prematurely, consolidates the client's progress towards goal attainment and helps to bring the bond to a mutually satisfying end (Ward, Chapter 10).

Now that I have presented the therapeutic alliance as an integrating framework for the rest of the book, we are in a position to move on to Chapters 2–10 — each of which deals with a key issue for counselling in action.

References

Beck, A.T., Rush, A.J., Shaw, B.F. and Emery, G. (1979) *Cognitive therapy of depression*. New York: Guilford.

Beutler, L.E., Crago, M. and Arizmendi, T.G. (1986) 'Therapist variables in psychotherapy process and outcome', in S.L. Garfield and A.E. Bergin (eds.), *Handbook of psychotherapy and behavior change* (3rd ed.). New York: Wiley.

Bordin, E.S. (1979) 'The generalizability of the psychoanalytic concept of the working alliance', *Psychotherapy: Theory, Research and Practice*, 16(3): 252–60.

Chaplin, J. (1988) *Feminist counselling in action*. London: Sage.

Clarkson, P. (1989) *Gestalt counselling in action*. London: Sage.

d'Ardenne, P. and Mahtani, A. (1989) *Transcultural counselling in action*. London: Sage.

Dorn, F.J. (ed.) (1984) *The social influence process in counseling and psychotherapy*. Springfield, IL: Charles C. Thomas.

Foreman, S.A. and Marmar, C.R. (1985) 'Therapist actions that address initially poor therapeutic alliances in psychotherapy', *American Journal of Psychiatry*, 142: 922–6.

Jacobs, M. (1988) *Psychodynamic counselling in action*. London: Sage.

Klerman, G.L. Weissman, M.M., Rounsaville, B.J. and Chevron, E.S. (1984) *Interpersonal psychotherapy of depression*. New York: Basic Books.

Luborsky, L., McLellan, A.T., Woody, G.E., O'Brien, C.P. and Auerbach, A. (1985) 'Therapist success and its determinants', *Archives of General Psychiatry*, 42: 602–11.

Maluccio, A.N. (1979) *Learning from clients: interpersonal helping as viewed by clients and social workers*. New York: Free Press.

Mearns, D. and Thorne, B. (1988) *Person-centred counselling in action*. London: Sage.

Moras, K. and Strupp, H.H. (1982) 'Pretherapy interpersonal relations, patients' alliance, and outcome in brief therapy', *Archives of General Psychiatry*, 39: 405–9.

Rachman, S.J. and Wilson, G.T. (1980) *The effects of psychological therapy* (2nd enlarged ed.). New York: Pergamon.

Stewart, I. (1989) *Transactional analysis counselling in action*. London: Sage.

Stiles, W.B., Shapiro, D.A. and Elliott, R. (1986) 'Are all psychotherapies equivalent?', *American Psychologist*, 41(2): 165–80.

Trower, P., Casey, A. and Dryden, W. (1988) *Cognitive-behavioural counselling in action*. London: Sage.

2 Structuring the Counseling Process

Robert W. Day and Richard T. Sparacio

Overview

This article defines structure and structuring in counseling and presents a rationale for its use in counseling. The facilitative, therapeutic, and protective functions of structure are explored; practical, consumer and process issues related to structure are described; the timing of structure in the therapeutic process is discussed; and limits and guidelines for structure and structuring in counseling and therapy are suggested. Rationale supporting the development of structuring skills by counselors is offered.

This article will advocate an active, but judicious use of structure in the counseling process by (a) defining structure and structuring; (b) describing the rationale for structuring; (c) discussing the facilitative, therapeutic, and protective functions of structuring; (d) delineating three themes that incorporate the major structuring issues; (e) discussing the proper timing of the introduction of structure in counseling; (f) identifying the limits and hazards of structure; and (g) providing some guidelines regarding the use of structure in counseling.

Structure and Structuring

Structure in counseling is defined as a joint understanding between the counselor and client regarding the characteristics, conditions, procedures, and parameters of counseling. *Structuring* refers to the interactional process by which *structure* is reached. *Structuring* is the means by which the counselor and client together define the guidelines that govern the counseling process, possibly involving such activities as informing, proposing, suggesting, recommending, negotiating, stipulating, contracting, and compromising.

This chapter is reprinted by kind permission of the American Association for Counseling and Development from the *Personnel and Guidance Journal* (1980), 59: 246–9.

Rationale for Counseling Structure

Although structure is fundamental to counseling, structuring is often a neglected dimension of the counseling process. However, all counseling is structured. Each counseling encounter can be described by its parameters, procedures, conditions, and characteristics. Structure cannot be avoided, but it can evolve or be developed. It can be perceived similarly or dissimilarly by client and counselor, impeding or enhancing the counseling process and outcome. The argument on behalf of structure is formulated on the following ideas: (a) structure should be developed rather than allowed to evolve; (b) the counselor's and client's perceptions of structure should be more rather than less similar, and (c) structure should be used to help accomplish counseling goals rather than being permitted to impede them.

More specific rationales in support of counseling structure include:

1 Any meaningful interaction will occur according to the guidelines that are assumed, adopted or established by the interactants. Therefore, all relationships (such as husband and wife, parent and child, student and teacher, and client and counselor) are founded and maintained by guidelines that may be generalized or idiosyncratic, explicit or implicit, dynamic or static. But, the guidelines do exist. The counselor/client coalition has at least two qualities, however, that distinguish its structure from that of other relationships: purpose (the relationship exists expressly for the purpose of benefiting the personal development of the client), and nature (the relationship is professional). As a result of the unique purpose and nature of counseling, customary social conventions are inappropriate and special norms, roles, responsibilities, and techniques apply (Headington, 1979). In this regard, Brammer and Shostrom (1977) have suggested that, 'paradoxical as it may seem, the provision of clear-cut limits provides the client with the power to move forward in therapy' (p. 194). This suggestion is based on the belief that 'the client's unfamiliarity with the counseling role may hinder the success of counseling' (Sue and Sue, 1977: 421).

2 Structure is regarded by several professionals in the area of counseling diverse populations (Lorion, 1974; Sue and Sue, 1977; Vontress, 1971) as an effective and necessary strategy in counseling minority clients. Keeping with this reasoning, Lorion (1974) proposed that 'although not presently a regular precursor of psychotherapy, some form of patient preparation early in screening merits further consideration' (p. 344).

Functions of Structure in Counseling

Structure serves three important functions in counseling:

1 It works in conjunction with the conduct of the counseling process.
2 It is therapeutic in and of itself.
3 It provides some degree of protection for both the client and the counselor.

Facilitative Function
Structure aids counseling in the following ways:

1 It serves to communicate and illustrate that the counselor has order and consistency in the conduct of counseling and conveys to the client how he or she is to be involved in the procedure. Brammer and Shostrom (1977) commented,

> Structuring provides the client with a framework or orientation for therapy. He [she] then feels that the relationship has a rational plan. Structure provides him [her] with a counseling road map and with a dossier of his [her] responsibilities for using the road map. (p. 192)

2 It reduces the amount, intensity, and impact of misunderstandings between counselor and client. These can result in either confusion or conflict, each of which can be detrimental to therapeutic progress. If preventative measures can be taken to reduce misunderstanding, counseling will be enhanced.
3 It provides a means by which differences in assumptions and expectations between counselor and client can be identified and resolved (Pietrofesa, Hoffman, Splete and Pinto, 1978; Stone and Stebbins 1975). Structuring helps to make implicit assumptions explicit and unspecified procedures specified. It establishes a procedure whereby either party can propose conditions or guidelines for the therapeutic relationship, through which agreement can be negotiated.
4 It is a means by which process ambiguity and client arousal, anxiety, initiative, and ingenuity can be regulated. Hansen, Stevic and Warner (1977) have advised that

> ambiguity in the counseling relationship can be very useful, but it must be controlled. . . . Ambiguity produces anxiety. . . . Although anxiety is an important part of effective therapy, there is an optimal level that each person can tolerate. If anxiety exceeds this point, the person will be so overwhelmed by anxiety that all of his [her] energies will be used in self preservation efforts, leaving no energy for therapeutic progress.

The authors suggested that in addition to the client,

> the counselor is subject to anxiety produced by ambiguity. There is less certainty and less control of the client's reactions in an ambiguous counseling relationship. (p. 260)

5 It renders counseling more efficient by specifying procedural variables and by providing a means through which procedure can be established.

That is, counseling is likely to proceed more smoothly and more orderly when there is a consensus between client and counselor as to how and for what reasons the process is to occur and the recognition of how that consensus can be altered.

6 It allows the counselor to feel more comfortable and confident (Pietrofesa et al., 1978). If the counselor has devoted some thought to the philosophy and methodology of his or her approach and has some idea of how to present these views and procedures to the client, then the counselor will be more self-aware and self-assured. Then more attention can be focused on the client and the client's concerns.

Therapeutic Function

Structure is therapeutic in that its process provides an incidental learning experience teaching the client a method by which other healthy and productive relationships can be developed. The therapeutic benefits of structure, therefore, include:

1 The experience of participating in a relationship that has been structured openly and adaptively thus enabling the client to observe himself or herself in a healthy relationship that she or he has had a role in constructing. Viewed from this perspective, structuring provides practice at formulating relationship goals, guidelines, and practice in translating these goals and guidelines into behaviors.

2 The client learns that it is realistic to expect some structure in all relationships, and that it is beneficial for the counselor and client to identify the structural basis of relationships.

3 Structuring helps the client who is misperceiving, distorting, or denying reality to identify and confront reality factors, at least in the counseling relationship (Edinberg, Zinberg and Kelman, 1975). Hansen, Stevic and Warner (1977) stated, for example, that 'a person with schizoid tendencies needs less ambiguity since he [she] is trying to maintain contact with reality; hence, a more structured situation is called for' (p. 260).

Protective Function

Structure can also serve to protect both participants in the therapeutic process by identifying the rights, roles, and obligations of counselor and client (Edinberg et al., 1975; Winborn, 1977). In fact, Stewart, Winborn, Johnson, Burks and Engelkes (1978) have maintained that it is the client's civil right to know what can be expected from counseling as practiced by his or her counselor.

Example of the Functions of Structure

Bixler (1949) provided an example of therapy that illustrates the functions of structure in the therapeutic setting in which the counselor was compelled to inform the client that harm of the counselor's person or property would not be permitted. In establishing this guideline, the counselor employed each of the facilitative, therapeutic, and protective functions of therapeutic structure.

1 By limiting the client's physical aggression, the counselor was able to maintain an accepting attitude toward the client and was able to continue a facilitative relationship.
2 The establishment of limits on the client's aggressive behavior communicated the reality of the need to control his physical aggression, insisting that, in the therapeutic situation, the counselor expected the client to assume that responsibility.
3 Requiring the client to refrain from acting out behaviors that would harm the counselor or his or her property, insured the counselor's right to not be harmed without infringing on the client's right to receive help and ventilate his aggression harmlessly.

Structure Themes in Counseling

Counselors differ in philosophy, theory, and methodology; agencies differ in policies and regulations; and clients differ in issues, needs, and backgrounds. Consequently, the structure of counseling will vary among counselors, agencies, and clients. However, there seem to be three structure themes that occur with sufficient regularity in counseling to merit counselor attention: practical issues, consumer issues, and process issues.

Practical Issues
Practical structuring is the procedure by which a joint understanding and agreement is reached between counselor and client on the logistical, pragmatic, and procedural aspects of the counseling situation. Practical issues include such topics as names and titles of participants; length of sessions; time of sessions; frequency of sessions; make-up of sessions; cancellation of appointments; crises and emergency contact; fees and fee payment procedures; referral; and consultation.

The structuring of practicalities is rather concrete, requires little time, and should be approached matter-of-factly. Practical structuring is often accomplished by secretarial or other support staff; but because these issues are central to the establishment and maintenance of the counseling relationship, it remains the counselor's responsibility to ensure that they are discussed satisfactorily.

An example of practical structuring is provided in the following counselor statement: 'So we have agreed, Carol, to meet for the time being every Monday at four in the afternoon. We'll have about forty-five minutes each session to talk over whatever is on your mind' (Benjamin, 1974: 17).

Consumer Issues

Consumer structuring is the procedure by which a joint understanding and agreement is reached between counselor and client on consumer-oriented concerns related to the counseling encounter. Consumer issues involve concerns such as confidentiality, taping or transcribing of sessions, record keeping, counselor qualifications, client's rights and responsibilities, counseling risks, potential for client success, cost of services, and therapeutic techniques. The following statement illustrates aspects of both practical and consumer structuring:

> I'm Mrs ——. You are probably not familiar with our counseling procedures here. From your application, you know our session is being taped. What is said is still private and confidential between us. We have 45 minutes and we'll use it in whatever way will benefit you. (Pietrofesa et al., 1978: 226)

Process Issues

Process structuring consists of the procedure by which a joint understanding and agreement is reached between counselor and client regarding the dynamics and methodology of the counseling encounter. Process issues entail a definition of counseling, indications of how to begin and end the therapeutic coalition and each counseling session, descriptions of counselor and client roles and responsibilities, identification of client goals, and information regarding referral, consultation, or follow-up.

An illustration of a statement of process structuring is taken from Stewart, Winborn, Johnson, Burks and Engelkes (1978):

> My job as a counselor is to listen and try to understand how you feel and think about things. I won't make decisions for you, but together we may come up with some things for you to consider in making a decision. If you make a decision, I will help you find ways to carry it out. Your part in counseling is to help me understand how you feel and think. You also have to make decisions and carry out the tasks that need doing before you can reach your goals. (p. 99)

Introducing Structure in the Therapeutic Process

Brammer and Shostrom (1977) suggest that

> with some clients who demand more structure or seem to be confused, formal structuring of the process must necessarily come early. With others, the formal structuring must come later. . . . With other clients who seem to take the process easily, a very minimum of formal structuring is necessary in the beginning. (p. 199)

Stewart et al. (1978) believe that

> if a client seems anxious, unsure, hesitant, or insecure, the counselor should provide structure immediately.... On the other hand a client may readily begin sharing a concern, and thus the provision of structure at this time would be an intrusion upon the client's desire to share the concern. If this is true, the counselor may provide structure at some later time in the initial interview. (p. 96)

We believe that formal structure should be provided for all referrals from professional referral sources and self-referrals who are being seen by the counselor for the first time. They believe structure is not necessary with clients who have already experienced it, or those who respond immediately to the counselor's open invitation to talk.

Although structuring may occur at any point in the therapeutic process, some structure should be provided at the initiation and termination of the helping relationship (Pietrofesa et al., 1978) and at the major transition points of counseling. Structure or restructure will also be needed when limits and procedures are violated, confusion or misunderstanding arises, or when concern for structure is expressed. The counselor must be flexible in structuring because it is not possible to anticipate everything needed to be structured, nor predict when it should be introduced (Bixler, 1949).

Limits and Guidelines for Structure and Structuring

Although structure is a fundamental component of the therapeutic relationship, the counselor should be aware of cautions and precautions that apply to the use of structure. The following limits and guidelines for structure and structuring are suggested.

1   Structure should be negotiated or requested, not coerced. Clients should be given the opportunity to respond and react to structure as well as to be able to modify it.
2   Structure, particularly restrictions and limitations, should not be applied for punitive reasons or in a punitive manner (Bixler, 1949).
3   The counselor should be aware of his or her rationale for structuring and should explain the reasons at the time of structuring or be prepared to provide rationale in response to the client's request for explanation.
4   The counselor should be guided by the client's readiness for structure and by the context of the relationship and process.
5   Too much or a too-rigid structure can be constraining for both the client and the counselor (Pietrofesa et al., 1978).
6   Ill-timed, lengthy, or insensitive structuring can result in client frustration or resistance (Benjamin, 1974), and can interrupt the continuity of the therapeutic process (Pietrofesa et al., 1978).
7   Unnecessary and purposeless recitation of rules and guidelines can imply that the counselor is more concerned with procedure than with

helpfulness. In fact, a compulsive approach to structuring can be indicative of low levels of counselor self-assurance (Hansen, Stevic and Warner, 1977).

8 The counselor must relate structure to the client's emotional, cognitive, and behavioral predisposition. For example, the highly independent individual or the isolate may be expected to resist what she or he interprets as personal threats or infringements. In such cases, structuring must be accomplished by sensitivity, tentativeness, and flexibility.

9 Structuring can 'imply that the relationship will continue with this particular client. It may turn out that the counselor will decide not to work with this client, or that the client may not be suitable for this counselor. Hence, the client or counselor may feel too committed to the relationship if it has been overstructured.' (Brammer and Shostrom, 1977: 194).

10 Structure cannot replace or substitute for therapeutic competence. Structure is not a panacea. It is not the total solution to building a productive therapeutic relationship. Structure is complementary and supplementary to human relations, communications, diagnostic, and intervention skills.

Responsibility for Structuring

Although results and process are the joint responsibility of counselor and the client, the ultimate responsibility for outcome is generally believed to be primarily that of the client; although the responsibility for process befalls the counselor. Outcome variables involve such factors as motivation, insight, risk, and adaptive behavior. Process variables include conditions of relationship, therapeutic techniques and strategies, and counseling structure. It is the counselor's responsibility, therefore, to ensure that structure is developed.

A more pragmatic reason for counselor responsibility in the provision of structure is that clients are predominantly problem and issue oriented. As a result their energies are bound in their concerns. They cannot be expected to be cognizant of the need for structure or the means by which to accomplish it, even in those cases where the client may sense that guidelines need be established.

Summary and Conclusion

This article has subscribed to the belief that structure is a significant, but often neglected, component of the therapeutic relationship. Structure was defined as the establishment of a joint understanding and agreement between the counselor and client regarding the characteristics, conditions, procedures, and parameters of counseling. Structuring was described as the process by which structure is attained, involving such activities as informing, proposing, suggesting, recommending, negotiating, stipulating, contracting, and compromising. A rationale for structure was based on the unique purpose and nature of the therapeutic relationship, and the use of structure as a strategy of preference for counseling minorities. The facilitative, therapeutic, and protective values of structure were discussed and illustrated; practical, consumer, and process issues were identified and examples of structuring statements in each area were provided. The timing of structuring was discussed; limits and guidelines for the use of structure and structuring were presented; and the counselor was identified as the individual responsible for structuring the counseling process.

Counselors are encouraged to contemplate structuring issues, practice structuring skills, acquire the ability to recognize counseling situations that require or can be enhanced by structure, and develop a structuring style and methodology. During counseling, structuring style should be developed rather than allowed to evolve. Counselor and client perceptions of structure should be more rather than less similar. It should be used to help accomplish counseling goals rather than be permitted to impede them.

References

Benjamin, A. (1974) *The helping interview* (2nd ed.). Boston: Houghton Mifflin.

Bixler, R.H. (1949) 'Limits are therapy', *Journal of Consulting Psychology*, 13: 1–11.

Brammer, L.M. and Shostrom, E.L. (1977) *Therapeutic psychology* (3rd ed.). Englewood Cliffs, NJ: Prentice-Hall.

Edinberg, G.M., Zinberg, N.E. and Kelman, W. (1975) *Clinical interviewing and counseling*. New York: Appleton-Century-Crofts.

Hansen, J.C., Stevic, R.R. and Warner, R.W., Jr. (1977) *Counseling theory and process* (2nd ed.). Boston: Allyn & Bacon.

Headington, B.J. (1979) *Communication in the counseling relationship*. Cranston, RI: Carroll Press.

Lorion, R.P. (1974) 'Patient and therapist variables in the treatment of low-income patients', *Psychological Bulletin*, 81: 344–54.

Pietrofesa, J.J., Hoffman, A., Splete, H.H. and Pinto, D.V. (1978) *Counseling: theory, research and practice*. Chicago: Rand-McNally.

Stewart, N.R., Winborn, B.B., Johnson, R.G., Burks, H.M., Jr. and Engelkes, J.R. (1978) *Systematic counseling*. Englewood Cliffs, NJ: Prentice-Hall.

Stone, G.L. and Stebbins L.W. (1975) 'Effect of differential pretraining on client self-disclosure', *Journal of Counseling Psychology*, 22: 17–20.

Sue, D.W. and Sue S. (1977) 'Barriers to effective cross-cultural counseling', *Journal of Counseling Psychology*, 24: 420–9.

Vontress, C.E. (1971) *Counseling negroes*. Boston: Houghton Mifflin.

Winborn, B.B. (1977) 'Honest labeling and other procedures for the protection of consumers of counseling', *Personnel and Guidance Journal*, 56: 206–9.

Discussion Issues

1 What do *you* consider to be the advantages and disadvantages of using structuring in your work with clients?
2 To what extent does your preferred approach to counselling recommend that you use structuring?
3 Under what conditions might you go counter to your preferred approach on this issue?
4 Which topics would you cover in your use of structuring with respect to (a) practical issues; (b) consumer issues; (c) process issues?
5 How specific would you be in delineating (a) your own tasks and (b) your clients' tasks in your use of structuring statements concerning process issues? (See Chapter 1 for a discussion of tasks in counselling).

3 Trust as an Underlying Dynamic in the Counseling Process: How Clients Test Trust

Margaret L. Fong and Barbara Gresbach Cox

Overview

Trust is a basic issue for clients entering into the counseling process. Counselors need to recognize and respond to clients' ways of testing trust.

Counselor training programs have been moving away from purely theoretical approaches to counseling in order to put more emphasis on counseling skills per se. A working knowledge of the core facilitative conditions was a much needed addition to the skills and knowledge repertoire of the counselor in training. In this process of transition, however, most training programs have focused attention on the smallest units of the counseling process in their skills-training courses such as primary empathy. Programs have lost the broader perspective of the give-and-take process events that shape the ongoing counselor–client relationship, such as social influence, resistance, and the development of trust.

The direct issue of how to foster trust has received little attention in counseling research, counselor training courses, and texts. Corrigan, Dell, Lewis and Schmidt (1980), in their monograph of research related to social influence, noted the lack of research on trustworthiness as a component of the influence process. Our search of other counseling research literature also revealed a dearth of direct references to trust. In a review of counseling texts on the market, we were surprised to find that only Egan (1982) included a separate discussion of trust, referenced in the index.

The current literature does, however, give some consideration to counseling as a holistic process and alludes to trust in this context. In his book *The Helping Process*, Brammer (1973) defined counseling as a series of interpersonal processes. He described the critical dimensions of

This chapter is reprinted by kind permission of the American Association for Counseling and Development from the *Personnel and Guidance Journal* (1983), 62: 163–6.

counseling as involvement–distance, ambiguity–clarity, and trust–distrust. He identified trust–distrust as the extent to which the client perceived that the counselor can be relied upon, and he considers this a crucial dimension that can help or hinder the relationship.

In the authors' experience, trust is one of the crucial issues in the first stage of counseling. Until clients can expose their innermost 'secrets' and make themelves vulnerable to the counselor, the real work of counseling cannot begin. If trust fails to develop, a client may terminate counseling prematurely, feeling that it is too threatening to risk significant self-disclosure with the counselor. Or the client may remain resistant and never share anything but superficial issues with the counselor.

Trust is the client's perception and belief that the counselor will not mislead or injure the client in any way. Strong (1968) stated that counselors were perceived to be trustworthy if they (a) had a reputation for honesty, (b) had a social role that was associated with trust (for example, a psychologist), (c) demonstrated sincerity and openness, and (d) showed no evidence of personal gain as a primary motivation for counseling.

The ability of clients to trust lies on a continuum, ranging from blind trust of any counselor who is perceived as an expert, to suspicion and distrust regardless of all evidence to the contrary. Most clients fall in the middle range. They are willing to trust a counselor until their trust is abused. Or, they will trust a counselor after they have put the counselor to the test. It is this testing process that will be discussed and described in this article.

How Trust Develops

How does trust develop? In normal friendships, two individuals grow to know and trust each other by spending time together in mutual activities, exchanging favors and help, and hearing confidences. In the counseling relationship, roughly the same process takes place, except that the same amount of time and range of activities are not available or possible. So, for trust to develop, the client must see observable instances of trust-worthiness. How clients handle this need to assess trustworthiness over a period of time is to formulate conscious and unconscious 'tests'. In a sense, clients gather empirical data to determine whether their working hypothesis ('This counselor is trustworthy') is valid.

When a counselor recognizes a client's tests of trust for what they are and learns to handle them skilfully, the counseling relationship is likely to develop smoothly and quickly, and the client will move into the working phase of counseling. If, on the other hand, the counselor misreads the client's covert attempts to begin the process of trust-building and responds to the client's overtures on a surface level, at best the result will be a delay in the further development of trust. If the counselor views the client's questions or statements as defensive, resistant, or hostile, he or she may respond negatively, so that the trust issue is evaded even further. This may even result in deterioration of the counseling relationship and termination of counseling. The counselor may never discover that the real issue was lack of trust.

Counselor Awareness of Trust

Beginning counselors are particularly prone to misconstrue the testing behaviors of clients and to deal directly with the overt content rather than the process of the counseling session. Each counselor needs to develop an 'ear' or awareness of when a client is testing trust. This comes, in large measure, from experience, because clients' testing behaviors are usually disguised. These situations can become opportunities for counselors to respond to the real issue at hand and to demonstrate to their clients that they can safely expose their problems to the counselor without fear of rebuff or emotional injury.

How Clients Test Trust

Certain client statements and behaviors seem to be used over and over again as tests of counselors' trustworthiness. The specific content of clients' questions and statements is unique to individual clients, but the general form that tests of trust take — for example, requesting information or telling a secret — are relatively predictable.

The form of a test a client presents seems to depend upon several factors. One is the time the client has been in the counseling process; that is, the initial session as opposed to the third or fourth sessions. Another factor is the client's preferred mode of gathering information; whether the client takes a cognitive approach or checks intuitive feelings. Perhaps the largest factor is the extent to which the client prefers direct versus indirect approaches to sensitive subject areas.

Common Tests of Counselors' Trustworthiness

As a way to assist new counselors to recognize client statements and behaviors that are potential tests of counselors' trustworthiness, the authors have identified and will describe six common types of client 'tests of trust.' These are: (a) requesting information, (b) telling a secret, (c) putting oneself down, (d) asking a favor, (e) inconveniencing the counselor, and (f) questioning the counselor's dedication and motivation. They have been organized for presentation in this article so that those tests of trust that tend to occur in the first sessions are discussed first. Table 3.1 summarizes these tests of trustworthiness.

Table 3.1 *Tests of trust on two levels*

Content: the client's test	Process: the real question
Information request	Can you understand-accept me?
Telling a secret	Can I be vulnerable with you?
Asking a favor	Are you reliable and honest?
Putting oneself down	Can you accept me?
Inconveniencing the counselor	Do you have consistent limits?
Questioning the counselor's motives	Is your caring real?

Requesting Information

Requests for information are an integral part of the client's interactions with the counselor. During the first session in particular, the client often asks about office hours, fees, counselor credentials, and how counseling works. Certain requests for information, however, may not be as straightforward as they seem. For example, the client may ask, 'Have you been married?' In such cases, a simple answer with a bit of elaboration might be: 'Yes, I've been married for ten years.' But this is rarely the answer the client is actually seeking. What the person may be wanting to know is 'Will you be able to understand my marital problem?' Or, 'Have you been married and divorced, and do you have enough personal experience to empathize with my pain?'

Clients sometimes ask, 'Are you a Christian?' Usually, instead of a simple yes or no, they want to know, 'Will you understand my values as a Christian?' 'Can I trust you to be supportive of me if you are (or are not) a Christian?'

Clearly then, to address the client's concern, the counselor needs to respond to the underlying questions with an answer that reflects the counselor's ability and willingness to accept and empathize with the client. In answer to the question about one's marital status, a more appropriate response might be, 'I guess you're wondering if I can understand how it feels to go through a divorce,' or '. . . to live on one's own as a divorced person.' A question about one's faith might be responded to with, 'I'm wondering if you're concerned that I'll judge you because of my faith.'

Telling a Secret

During the initial counseling sessions, the client is usually acutely aware of the counselor's nonverbal behaviors, interpreting them (probably unconsciously) in terms of the counselor's openness to and acceptance of the client. In assessing the trustworthiness of the counselor, the client may ask for information and inquire directly about confidentiality. Other clients may be indirect. They may test whether it is safe to reveal highly personal aspects of their private lives to the counselor. Clients ask themselves, 'Is it right to be vulnerable with this person?'

One way of testing this is to send up a trial balloon by telling the counselor a secret — not just any secret, nor even one germane to the client's presenting problem. Usually it involves some behavior of the client or the client's family that may have embarrassment or shame attached to it.

Examples of secrets a client may offer are, 'Sometimes I masturbate,' 'When my baby keeps crying in the middle of the night, I hate being a mother,' or 'My brother is an alcoholic.'

What is confusing to most counselors is that the secret is usually presented unexpectedly and generally does not relate directly to the logical flow of communication in the session. This new information may represent a totally new and unexpected topic. Moreover, the secret offered may be at a much higher level of self-disclosure than has yet been risked by the client.

Often, the secret that is being used to test the counselor involves an area that tends to be uncomfortable to discuss or is marginally taboo, such as deviant sexual practices. This unexpected or potentially difficult knowledge about the client can jar the counselor temporarily. The counselor's first reaction might be, 'What am I going to do with this?' or 'Why did you have to tell me that? I really don't want to know it.'

If the counselor becomes perceptibly defensive in reaction to the client's revelation or makes some statement that seems to be judgmental, the client is almost certain to decide that it is unsafe to be vulnerable with this person. The level of trust drops. And further self-disclosure of any depth may not be forthcoming, at least for a very long time. The client may perceive judgment and censure in even innocent counselor responses, such as 'Do you really do that?' or 'Did that actually happen?'

The counselor can deal effectively with this test of trust by remembering that the offering of this secret is really a question: 'Are you safe to be vulnerable with?' The more effective counselors' responses in these situations are simple reflections of feelings and neutral, but warm responses. By reflecting a client's feelings, the counselor conveys, 'I have heard you, and I can talk about your problems without reacting negatively or judgmentally.' It is inadvisable to actively probe the client's concerns surrounding the secret at this point. The secret may serve primarily as a useful device — a test — and not be a core concern for the client.

At this juncture in the session, the level of self-disclosure has risen sharply and unexpectedly — and it is the client who should set the pace for a time. The counselor should let the client guide the discussion that follows. If the client wants to express or divulge more about the circumstances related to the secret, the counselor's neutral but accepting responses will allow this. Often the client looks relieved when the secret has been told, and this critical passage in the relationship has been satisfactorily negotiated. The client now feels more reassured that the counselor is trustworthy, even with secrets. Generally, the client will then proceed to discuss issues more relevant to his or her counseling needs.

Asking a Favor

Clients frequently ask their counselors to perform favors for them. Some of the requests are reasonable, some are inappropriate to the counselor–client relationship, and some represent unreasonable demands on the counselor. All requests of clients for a favor should be viewed, especially initially, as potential tests of trust. In the first counseling sessions particularly, the counselor needs to be sensitive to requests that may be more important as tests of trust than as an actual desire to receive something or have a service done.

When new clients ask a favor, the simple granting or denying of the favor is probably not the primary issue. Of main importance is how the counselor handles the request, whether the counselor's response is given helpfully, how honest the counselor seems to be in demonstrating a willingness to accommodate the client, and how reliably the counselor follows through.

If a favor is a reasonable one, and the counselor is willing to do it, it is critical that the favor be followed through and honored as promised. The counselor must be sure to remember, for example, to bring the book from home to the next session, or complete the insurance form and mail it in on time. When the client's request is handled appropriately, the client can accept the counselor's sincere willingness to help. If the counselor fails to remember to perform the favor agreed to, the client has tangible proof that the counselor is unreliable, does not care very much, and therefore cannot be trusted.

The favor requested may be inappropriate in the counselor's view. The counselor may find it an overextension of the relationship to attend a client's graduation, participate in a social function given by the client, or lend the client an expensive biofeedback unit, for example. In such cases, the favor should not be granted and the counselor's reason for not granting the favor should be directly but tactfully conveyed to the client. It is very important that the reason not be camouflaged by excuses ('I'll be away that weekend,' or 'I've promised the feedback unit to someone else this week'). It is just as damaging to the client's trust to grant a favor grudgingly or to evade the favor dishonestly as it is to fail to follow through on a promised favor.

A 'no' from a counselor in response to a request can actually be constructive to the relationship. When handled skillfully, it demonstrates that the counselor keeps the relationship honest, can be counted on to do what is best for the client, and is consistently sincere. A client might ask, 'Could you call my office and tell my boss I'm seeing a counselor?' An appropriate answer could be, 'I think it's important for you to try talking directly to your boss.' After this, the ramifications of the situation for the client can be explored.

The counselor who grants favors appropriately in a counselor–client relationship, who knows how to say 'yes' at the right times and 'no' at the right times, and who knows how to be sincere and supportive in the process, is a counselor who can be trusted.

Putting Oneself Down

Putting oneself down is a form of testing the counselor's basic acceptance. Clients who test their counselor by putting themselves down usually do so in the first or second session. What the client is really doing is asking 'Can you accept the real me, no matter what others think?' Acceptance is seen by clients as a critical component of trustworthiness.

This form of testing trust is done by making statements or asking rhetorical questions designed to shock the counselor. Clients sometimes describe how inadequate or bad they are and then carefully watch the counselor's verbal and nonverbal reactions. Examples of putting down oneself are statements such as, 'No one can believe how many times I've messed up,' or questions like, 'Why can't I ever seem to remember my child's medicine?' Putting oneself down can also take the form of the client reciting a litany of past negative behaviors. Some clients may matter-of-factly tell about suicide attempts that they have made, for example. Younger clients may recount the fights they have been in at school. Like all tests of trust in counseling, the client's questions or statements are not intended to be taken at face value. They are designed to measure the counselor's acceptance and trustworthiness.

This test tends to occur so early in counseling that the counselor may not have enough information about the client to make a realistic assessment regarding the truth of the statements. Counselors need to respond to clients' self-put-downs in a neutral manner. Counselors should neither agree that such clients are inadequate nor try to persuade them to view themselves more positively. What the counselor can convey is a reply that says, 'I am interested in you and your problems.' For example, the counselor might reply to a litany of the client's negative behaviors, 'It sounds like you've had a lot of rough experiences that have affected you. I'm open to talking about any of your concerns. I'm interested in helping you work out your problems.'

In responding to the client's self-put-downs, the counselor reflects to the client what the counselor has heard and then responds with statements of interest and acceptance. If the counselor makes the mistake of reacting either positively or negatively to the clients' descriptions of their 'bad' behavior early in the relationship, trust is unlikely to be built. Clients will see the counselor as potentially judgmental or opinionated and not a safe person with whom to share their most vulnerable thoughts and feelings.

Inconveniencing the Counselor

Whether clients can trust their counselor also depends on their perception that the counselor can be counted on to set limits or boundaries in the relationship. Clients need to know that there will be no exploitation in any of the counselor–client interactions because the counselor will provide structure and set limits on the give-and-take between them. Parents of adolescents are very familiar with this concept because they learn through experience that setting limits provides the foundation for security and trust.

Like the adolescent, the client can test this aspect of trust by attempting to inconvenience the counselor. Often impositions upon the counselor take the form of forgetfulness or unreasonable demands related to appointments. The client may change the appointment once, then twice, and on the second occasion not show up at the agreed-upon time. Another client may show up an hour early and request to be seen at that time '. . . since I'm already here.'

Inconveniencing the counselor can take several forms, such as asking whether the client's child may sit in '. . . because I couldn't find a baby-sitter.' The client may push the limits of appropriateness by bringing a sack lunch and saying, 'I hope you don't mind if I eat, I missed lunch today so I could come here.' Or the client may ask, 'Could I make a few quick phone calls on your telephone before we start? I really need to call the office.' Such tests of trust usually take the form of extension of ordinary privileges, causing the counselor minor inconvenience or otherwise creating annoying situations.

Although some of these behaviors, such as missed appointments, can sometimes be interpreted as resistance on the part of the client, behaviors like changing appointments or showing up unexpectedly, are more likely to represent tests of the counselor that ask, 'Do you have limits and stand by them?' and 'Do you maintain your self-respect?' In such instances, the issue of trust is one the counselor needs to focus on rather than the behavior itself.

The counselor, knowing that the client is engaged in a test of trust by checking limits, needs to clarify once again the role of the counselor in the counselor relationship. Certain elements of the counseling process, such as appointment policies, the need for an environment with few distractions, and any other personal counselor preferences (i.e. no smoking) should be discussed directly and genuinely.

The consequences to clients when they fail to abide by counseling policies should be discussed in advance of enforcing them. For example, if the counselor's agency drops a client from the active list onto a waiting list after two missed appointments, the client should be told in advance of the consequences of missed appointments.

When counselors respond directly to attempts of clients to inconvenience them, counselors demonstrate that they have boundaries, can be counted on to set personal limits, and thus will probably honor any limits that clients need to have respected. This knowledge strengthens the clients' perceptions, also based on other kinds of evidence, that their counselor is trustworthy.

Questioning the Counselor's Motives

As Strong (1968) defined trust, one important element is the perception on the part of the person that the other person in a relationship is not getting any personal gain at the expense of the other. In the counseling relationship, this concern may be framed by the client as a mental question, 'What is this person getting out of listening to all my troubles?' Clients may not have experienced many genuinely caring people in their lives. They often believe that it is a 'dog-eat-dog' world where one must be on guard or be exploited. It is confusing to such a client, then, to enter into a relationship with a counselor who seems to care genuinely. Suspicious clients ask themselves, 'Is this just a facade to get me to keep coming back for the fees I pay?' 'What do I really mean to this counselor?'

Rarely does a client ask these questions as clearly and directly as they are formulated in the client's mind. Instead, the client poses a series of thinly veiled inquiries that are intended to test the counselor's motives for doing this kind of professional work. Typically, the client asks a number of such questions, interspersed throughout the session. Unless counselors are alert to the fact that this is a form of testing trust, they may fail to respond adequately to the crucial issue: that is, the client's need to be seen as a worthwhile human being in the counselor's eyes and not just as a source of income for the counselor. It is critical that the counselor recognize that the client is really asking. 'What do I mean to you? Am I just your job, or do you see me as a person worth caring about?'

A typical series of queries and statements might be, 'I'll bet you have a lot of clients.' 'You probably see a lot of people worse off than me.' 'How can you manage to keep us all straight? Don't you mix us up?' 'I'll bet it's really hard for you to hear problems all day and not take them home with you.' A final question – one which really puts the client's vulnerability on the line – may be, 'Do you think about me between sessions?' When artificially placed in sequence together like this, it becomes clear that the client is wondering, 'Exactly what do I mean to you?' and 'Is your caring real?' In other words, many clients want their counselor to make explicit the motivations for being in the counseling profession in general, and for helping them, as unique individuals, in particular.

To adequately respond to this test, the counselor has to be both genuine and willing to disclose attitudes and feelings about the client and the rewards of being a counselor. The counselor might begin by noting the theme the client is expressing. Example responses are, 'You've asked me several times about my caseload. I guess you wonder how clearly I see your situation. What stands out for me about you...' or 'If I were you I might be wondering does this busy counselor really care? Now might be a good time for me to sum up my concerns and hopes for you.' In both examples the counselor reflects the real concern and then immediately provides a clear statement of the client's uniqueness.

Each counselor experiences both rewards and some hassles from being in the profession. A statement like, 'You're right, some days I see many clients. What I've found that keeps me going is . . .' or 'One of the things I've learned about being a counselor is that I really value . . .', can lead into a discussion about the rewards of counseling or the difference between caring and overinvolvement.

When the counselor honestly responds to the client's concern about personal motives, the client gets information that supports trust. The client decides that the counselor is human, is clear about the gains from counseling, really does care, and can be trusted.

Conclusion

Counselor training programs have taught counseling skills in terms of concrete counselor responses to the client in interview situations rather than overall process and relationship dimensions. Counselors need to be aware of these larger dimensions, such as trust, that are critical to the development of the counseling relationship. The development of trust can be conceived of as a series of relationship interchanges between the client and the counselor. These interchanges, which we have labeled as tests of trust, are quite predictable in form and can be responded to by the counselor in ways that directly enhance or disrupt trust building. By using the framework we have described, the counselor can recognize potential tests of trust and respond effectively to the covert or overt client message, 'Can I trust you?'

References

Brammer, L.M. (1973) *The helping process*. Englewood Cliffs, NJ: Prentice-Hall.

Corrigan, J.D., Dell, D.M., Lewis, K.N. and Schmidt, L.D. (1980) 'Counseling as a social influence process: a review', *Journal of Counseling Psychology*, 27: 395–441.

Egan, G. (1982) *The skilled helper: model, skills, and methods for effective helping* (2nd ed.). Monterey, CA: Brooks/Cole.

Strong, S.R. (1968) 'Counseling: An interpersonal influence process', *Journal of Counseling Psychology*, 15: 215–24.

Discussion Issues

1   How have your clients tended to test their trust in you as their counsellor? How did you respond to these tests and what happened subsequently?

2   What happened when you dealt *at face value* with your clients' communications that Fong and Cox would regard as implying tests of trust? What do you think would have happened if you had responded to these communications as such tests?

3   Have any of your clients prematurely terminated the counselling relationship because of lack of trust in you as their counsellor? In retrospect, how might you have handled the situation differently?

4   What influence do you think that the gender and race of counsellors have on the trust-testing behaviour of clients of (a) the same gender/race and (b) different gender/race? What have been your own experiences as a counsellor with respect to this issue?

5   If you have been or are currently in personal therapy did you (and if so, how did you) test your trust in your therapist/ counsellor? How did he or she respond and what was the outcome?

4 Helping the Reluctant Client to Engage in Counselling

Robert J. Manthei and David A. Matthews

Overview

The reluctant or resistant counselling client is a common though frustrating client for many counsellors. A number of techniques designed to aid reluctant clients to engage in the process of counselling are described.

While most counsellors would agree that all clients should enter counselling voluntarily and free from all forms of coercion and threat, it is nevertheless common for counsellors to find themselves faced with clients who may need and desire help, but are involuntary, resistant to, or reticent about engaging in the process of counselling. Faced with these clients, counsellors can choose to accept the reluctance at face value, that is, as an unequivocal refusal to help. Alternatively, they can sensitively and non-judgementally attempt to engage the client in order that the real meaning of the reluctance may become clear. It may well be that many reluctant clients need only to find genuineness, reassurance, and the right invitation from a counsellor to begin a relationship.

Although given brief mention in most standard counselling texts (see, for example, Belkin, 1975; Brammer, 1979; Brown and Brown, 1977; Hamblin, 1974; Munro et al., 1979; Patterson, 1974), resistant, reluctant or involuntary counselling clients remain unsolved riddles to most counsellors. Even the numerous attempts that have been made to clarify both the process of counselling and the teaching of counselling skills (for example, Carkhuff and Pierce, 1977; Egan, 1975; Ivey and Gluckstern, 1974; Kagan, 1975) have included only brief discussions of specific techniques that could be used to engage reluctant clients in the process of

This chapter is reprinted (with slight modification) by kind permission of Hobsons Press Publishing PLC from the *British Journal of Guidance and Counselling* (1982), 10(1): 44–50.

counselling; the same is true of Calia and Corsini's (1973) critical-incidents approach to counselling.

By contrast, Vriend and Dyer's (1973) discussion of reluctant clients is a comparatively thorough discussion of the forms of reluctance, of possible reasons for reluctance, and of strategies for counselling reluctant clients. Their suggestions for dealing with such clients include:

(a) questioning the source of the reluctance;
(b) dealing with the behaviour as it is manifested;
(c) interpreting the reluctance;
(d) exploring with the client his/her circumstances;
(e) explaining the counselling process;
(f) negotiating mutually-agreed behaviour contracts.

Accepting the widely-held view that successful counselling of necessity involves some degree of voluntary client participation (Patterson, 1974; Vriend and Dyer, 1973), this article expands Vriend and Dyer's list of techniques designed to aid reluctant clients to engage in the process of their own counselling. Implicit in any discussion of techniques for engaging reluctant clients is the necessity for counsellors to be patient, open-minded, and creative in their approach to reluctant clients. When working with such clients, it is essential to allow them time to feel comfortable and develop trust, to refrain from pre-judging clients' moods/motives/needs, and to try out more than the normal variety of invitations to talk or participate.

The techniques discussed below are categorised as follows: (1) interpreting the client's silence; (2) encouraging non-verbal responding; (3) working at the client's pace; (4) responding to the talkative reluctant client; and (5) explaining the counselling process. The authors have had success with all of the techniques in actual counselling relationships. It should be stressed, however, that counsellors must decide for themselves when it is appropriate to use these techniques. In all cases they should be used tentatively, sensitively and with due concern for the real needs of the client. As with all counselling techniques, they are open to abuse and misuse, and counsellors should regularly monitor how frequently they are being used and for what purposes.

1. Interpreting the Client's Silence

Initially, confronted with a client's silence, the counsellor should try to assess what the silence means for the client, and some of the reasons for the behaviour. The following techniques describe ways in which the counsellor might begin to do this.

(a) Silence can express many things; anger, fear, boredom, contempla-
tion, reverence, respect, embarrassment, solitude, sadness, contempt,

defence, hostility. Silence may also indicate that the client does not understand the language the counsellor is using. Since it can mean so many things, there is a risk in judging too quickly what a particular silence means. Counsellors should make every attempt to understand, and become more sensitive to, the possible meanings of silence.

(b) In doing this, particular attention should be paid to the client's movements, gestures, and physical appearance. Counsellors should attend to these feeling indicators and comment on them, even though the client might not respond. Simply reporting what is observed can result in the client agreeing with or correcting the observation. Either way, the client has been engaged.

(c) Interpreting clients' feelings can also be accomplished by written means. For example, when clients do not respond verbally, they may respond to a written observation or a simple drawing. When using written messages, counsellors should write simply and briefly, in large letters and in full view of the client. Such messages can usefully be supplemented with drawings. For example, the counsellor could write a simple message such as 'How are you feeling?', and draw two faces, one sad and one happy. The client is then free to respond to either of these techniques in a minimal, safe way. With imagination, this sort of communication can be continued until the client feels secure enough to interact verbally. When this technique has been used, typical reactions have varied from interested, though minimal, non-verbal responses (a gesture or pointing to the appropriate face), to obvious amusement and a fuller response (talking or writing/drawing a follow-up message). Seldom have clients failed to respond in some significant way to this form of communication.

(d) Mirroring as a form of interpretation can be used to highlight dominant aspects of the client's behaviour. In this technique, counsellors imitate movements, gestures, or postures that seem meaningful. Counsellors should realise that mirroring can be a provocative form of interpretation, and may elicit a strong response, positive or negative. Such responses tend to be unpredictable but may include anger and denial ('That's not me!'), resistance ('That's me if *you* say so!'), acceptance ('That's me all right'), and understanding ('If that is me, I want to change'). Some clients immediately recognise a game they have been playing and abandon it, becoming more willing to relate honestly.

2. Encouraging Non-verbal Responding

Although similar to some of the interpretation-of-silence techniques, the following suggestions are intended to encourage the client to initiate exploration and self-disclosure without having to verbalise thoughts or feelings. They are invitations to interact rather than counsellor interpretations of client behaviour.

(a) It is often effective to invite clients to draw or write thoughts or feelings they find hard to verbalise. Doing this may enable them to clarify their thoughts or feelings, when spoken words would be impossible or inadequate.

(b) A more structured exercise would involve asking clients to write a slogan that typifies how they see themselves or present themselves to others. If they seem interested, but reluctant to act, counsellors could offer their own interpretation, watching closely to gauge clients' reactions to this form of feedback. For example, the counsellor might write a slogan such as 'Kick me' or 'I don't understand'. If carried further, such simple descriptions usually contain additional messages that are kept hidden. Often they clarify the first message. To illustrate, 'Kick me' might be followed by 'I like it', and 'I don't understand' followed by 'It's safer that way'. This technique is based on the Transactional Analysis concept of 'sweatshirts' — an ulterior message communicated to others that usually involves a game (see James and Jongeward, 1975). Once the game or ulterior message is understood, more constructive ways of communicating can result. Most clients, even angry and defensive ones, will be interested enough in this form of information about themselves to continue the interaction with the counsellor in some way. A variation of this technique is for the client to complete sentences presented by the counsellor. For example, 'When I go to work, I feel...' and 'When meeting new people, I usually...'. Clients can complete these sentences by themselves and then talk about them when they are ready.

(c) If the client is willing, there are a number of problem/attitude/feeling checklists that can be used to enable clients to indicate areas of concern. However, if clients will fill out a checklist, they will usually interact with the counsellor in other ways. An example of a problem checklist is the Mooney Problem Checklist (Gordon and Mooney, 1950).

(d) Clients can be encouraged to express thoughts or feelings physically; for example, by acting, miming, or posturing. Almost any verbal message can be communicated physically in a way that makes the meaning more clear and direct. The counsellor's tasks are to be persuasive enough to encourage clients to express themselves nonverbally, and perceptive enough to understand the meaning of such actions.

(e) Having once engaged clients to act out thoughts or feelings, counsellors should have them exaggerate specific behaviours. Repeating a gesture with emphasised movement may aid clients to clarify its meaning and the personal feelings that lie behind it.

3. Working at the Client's Pace

Many counsellors, pressed by time and institutional demands, quickly become frustrated with reluctant clients. Whether expressed verbally by the counsellor or not, clients will sense this frustration from a variety of cues: facial expressions, voice cues, and non-verbal actions. Therefore, it is essential that counsellors exercise patience and open-mindedness with reluctant clients. Counsellors must accept the fact that these clients need more time. In some cases, dealing with the reluctance indirectly will foster trust and the development of an appropriate relationship.

(a) Counsellors should try taking reluctant clients for a walk; giving them some small non-counselling task to do; allowing them to remain while the counsellor continues with other work. In these situations, counsellors should always explain what they are doing and why. The initial focus does not always have to be on the reluctant client's problem. The client may simply need time to get to know and trust the counsellor enough to begin talking.

(b) Clients can be asked to bring photographs of self, family or friends, that they are willing to share. Even if they refuse to discuss the photos they bring, clients have been engaged in a significant way. Some of the techniques described earlier can then be used to comment on and interpret photo contents.

(c) Another means of structuring initial sessions with reluctant clients, similar to techniques used by Hamblin (1974) and Rainbow (1977), is for counsellors to invite clients to respond to situational cards which depict certain life situations. For example, pictures or cartoons depicting a happy family scene or a typical recreational situation can be used. Counsellors should prompt clients to respond by asking such questions as: 'What do you see?' 'How does this make you feel?' 'How is this like your situation?' Typical reactions to this technique have ranged from indifference and/or confusion ('Dunno, can't see anything there'), to tears and/or distress ('Our family is *never* like that one!'), to understanding and insight ('Yes, that's Dad: that's really like him'). Whatever the response, the counsellor has learned more about the client.

(d) If clients are agreeable, they can be given some small task to perform before the next session. A bit of 'homework' may encourage them to cooperate long enough to see what the counsellor has in mind. An example of a homework suggestion would be to ask clients to keep brief diaries of certain behaviours, thoughts, or feelings until the next session. The purpose of the homework should be described, emphasising that sharing the contents is entirely voluntary.

(e) If things do not progress well, the counsellor can try changing seating positions and/or activities. Examples are swapping chairs with the client, moving to another room, beginning another activity. In some cases a mere change of position or activity will result in clients being more willing to interact.

4. Responding to the Talkative Reluctant Client

Not all reluctant clients are silent clients. Some will readily verbalise feelings such as anger and hostility, or interact in over-compliant or evasive ways. The effect is the same: avoidance of meaningful contact with the counsellor. Most of the suggestions listed below involve interpretative or confrontative qualities, and counsellors should avoid using them in an aggressive, interrogating manner.

(a) As in the case of the silent client, counsellors should pay particular attention to the talkative client's movements, gestures and physical appearance. These factors may reveal information about the client's circumstances that can be commented on directly or used to interpret the talkativeness.

(b) The manner in which a client speaks may reveal as much as what is actually said. Since the voice contains many clues as to a person's feeling state and beliefs, counsellors should be sensitive to voice quality and use such information in framing a response.

(c) In many instances it will be productive to have clients repeat particular statements, phrases, or words. This repetition, preferably with added emphasis, can serve to highlight underlying feelings and to clarify meanings.

(d) Counsellors should notice when clients use 'need' when what is really meant is 'want'. Seldom do clients need something/someone in order to continue functioning. 'Need' implies helplessness, while 'want' implies autonomy and the ability to change. This difference can be pointed out, and clients asked to repeat their statement using the appropriate word. Similar attention can be given to differences between 'you' and 'I', 'we' and 'me', 'can't' and 'won't'. The intention is to have clients personalise their statements and take responsibility for them.

(e) The counsellor can point out to clients the difference between speaking in the 'passive' voice and the 'active' voice. Use of the passive voice implies that the client is being controlled by others. Use of the active voice places responsibility and power to control where it belongs, with the client.

(f) Discrepant behaviours can be pointed out in a non-judgemental manner, for example, where what clients say conflicts with what they do, or where what they say conflicts with what they feel or how they look. While many counsellors feel this confrontation technique is risky, some risk often has to be taken with reluctant clients to avoid losing them altogether. In taking such risks, counsellors should act on their 'hunches' about underlying messages and feelings by checking their accuracy with the client.

(g) If video-tape equipment is readily available, clients can be asked to view themselves and comment on what they see. This situation may be threatening for some, but at the same time, it allows both counsellor and client to refer to more objective evidence to explain their observations.

5. Explaining the Counselling Process

In some cases, clients' reluctance to engage in counselling can be largely overcome by explaining the counselling process, how it works, and what the client can expect from the counsellor. Not only does every client have a right to this information, but such client role-induction has been shown to result in enhanced outcomes (Orlinsky and Howard, 1978).

(a) In using any of the previously discussed suggestions, it is important that counsellors 'think aloud'; that is, explain what they are doing and why. The mere fact that counsellors are prepared to reveal their motives, intentions, thoughts, and feelings, can act as an incentive and model for the client to do likewise.

(b) Similarly, counsellors should explain the process of counselling to clients in simple, non-technical language that demystifies the process. Doing this with all clients, not just reluctant clients, may help to assuage clients' fears, doubts and hesitations about the process of counselling.

Conclusion

This list is not to be considered exhaustive. The suggestions we have outlined should be regarded as possibilities which indicate the range of counsellor behaviours that are possible if the reluctant or difficult client is approached with patience, open-mindedness, sensitivity and creativity. We wish to add, however, that failure to engage a reluctant client is not necessarily the counsellor's failure. Provided counsellors are sensitive, perceptive and creatively responsive when working with reluctant clients, they do not have to feel that they ought to be able to work effectively with every non-voluntary client they encounter.

References

Belkin, G.S. (1975) *Practical counseling in the schools*. Dubuque, IA: Brown.
Brammer, L.M. (1979) *The helping relationship* (2nd ed.) Englewood Cliffs, NJ: Prentice-Hall.

Brown, J.H. and Brown, C.S. (1977) *Systematic counseling*. Champaign, IL: Research Press.

Calia, V.F., and Corsini, R.J. (1973) *Critical incidents in school counseling*. Englewood Cliffs, NJ: Prentice-Hall.

Carkhuff, R.R. and Pierce, R.M. (1977) *The art of helping: trainer's guide*. Amherst, MA: Human Resource Development Press.

Egan, G. (1975) *The skilled helper*. Monterey, CA: Brooks/Cole.

Gordon, L.V. and Mooney, R.L. (1950) *The Mooney problem checklist*. New York: Psychological Corporation.

Hamblin, D.H. (1974) *The teacher and counselling*. Oxford: Blackwell.

Ivey, A.E. and Gluckstern, N.B. (1974) *Basic attending skills*. North Amherst, MA: Microtraining Associates.

James, M. and Jongeward, D. (1975) *The people book: transactional analysis for students*. Menlo Park, CA: Addison-Wesley.

Kagan, N. (1975) *Interpersonal process recall: a method of influencing human interaction*. East Lansing, MI: Michigan State University.

Munro, E.A., Manthei, R.J. and Small, J.J. (1979) *Counselling: a skills approach*. Wellington, New Zealand: Methuen.

Orlinsky, D.E. and Howard, K.I. (1978) 'The relation of process to outcome in psychotherapy' in S.L. Garfield and A.E. Bergin (eds.), *Handbook of psychotherapy and behavior change: an empirical analysis* (2nd ed.). New York: Wiley.

Patterson, C.H. (1974) *Relationship counseling and psychotherapy*. New York: Harper & Row.

Rainbow, C. (1977) *Support group*. Health Education Council Project 12–18. Cambridge: Cambridge University Press.

Vriend, J. and Dyer, W.W. (1973) 'Counseling the reluctant client', *Journal of Counseling Psychology*, 20(3): 240–6.

Discussion Issues

1 How have your reluctant clients manifested their reluctance to engage in the counselling process? How did you attempt to deal with this issue and with what effects?

2 Think of instances in your own life when you were reluctant to engage in an activity or process. How do you account for your reluctance? To what extent can you use your experience to help you understand the experiences of your reluctant clients?

3 How have you honestly felt when clients show their reluctance to engage in the counselling process? How have you dealt with your feelings?

4 In retrospect how might you have responded differently to reluctant clients whom you have failed to engage in the counselling process?

5 Under what conditions might you not attempt to engage reluctant clients in the process of counselling?

5 The Evaluation of Counselling: A Goal-Attainment Approach

Carole Sutton

Overview

There exist a great many models of counselling: person-centred approaches, transactional analysis, rational-emotive approaches, and many others. There is a shortage of means of evaluating these and other models of counselling — particularly from the point of view of the client or customer. This paper considers possible ways of evaluating counselling, and describes a goal-attainment approach being developed at Leicester by Professor Martin Herbert and Carole Sutton in which the *client* is the evaluator of the service offered.

Readers of this paper will be aware of the wide range of 'models of counselling' which exist, and of the confusion which they can present both to people seeking counselling help and to those seeking counselling training. It was eight years ago (Sutton, 1979) that I quoted Patterson's comments upon the state of counselling and psychotherapy in 1977,

> Anything goes now in psychotherapy. The field is a mess...Every few months we have a new technique or approach being advocated in books and journal articles. But what is discouraging — and disturbing — is the lack of, or the inadequacy of, theory and concepts supporting the new methods or techniques; the ignoring, or ignorance of, the research...the evangelistic fervour with which many of the approaches are advocated...the failure to recognise that what is called counselling or psychotherapy can be for better or worse — that people can be hurt as well as helped!

I do not think that things have improved since that time. If anything, not only has the multiplicity of models increased, but those being trained in counselling are learning the particular model favoured by their trainers; this can bring major difficulties both for counselling trainees and for clients.

This chapter is reprinted by kind permission of the British Association for Counselling from *Counselling* (1987), 60: 14–20.

First, for counsellors: how does a student or trainee who has been taught, say, the person-centred approach, communicate with those using principles of, say, transactional analysis? How do counsellors versed in psycho-analytic theory communicate with social learning theorists? I suggest, with difficulty.

Secondly, and more importantly, for clients: does it *really* not matter whether a person seeking help finds himself or herself with a person trained in any of the different 'schools' of counselling? Are people really just as likely to be helped with their difficulties of living and relationships by *any* counsellor? The evidence, I suggest, from Truax and Carkhuff (1967), is to the contrary: people can indeed be harmed as well as helped. It is time that we as counsellors and counselling trainers put our house in order.

In the remainder of this paper I wish to discuss three areas in turn.

1   To consider, briefly, research findings concerning helpful counselling, and to endorse them.
2   To describe the model of evaluating counselling which Professor Martin Herbert and I are developing at Leicester.
3   To clarify that the model may be used with *any* theoretical orientation to counselling.

Research Findings Concerning Helpful Counselling

In the state of confusion which I have described earlier, perhaps one way out is do what any psychologist is trained to do: go to the literature. What *does* the research have to say about evaluated counselling approaches which help rather than harm?

In my view the literature, particularly the extensive review published by Truax and Carkhuff (1967), suggests the value of a broad-based 'person-centred' approach, and that whatever else is offered, people seeking help should be met by counsellors who extend to them *accurate empathy, non-possessive warmth and genuineness*.

There are those who have questioned (for example, Rachman and Wilson, 1980) the value of this 'therapeutic triad', but there are many who conclude with humanistic psychologists like Carl Rogers, Abraham Maslow and John Rowan that this approach to people contains something of enduring value. It is an approach which many believe will stand the test of time. It is, however, only the beginning.

Thereafter, then, what else? I have suggested elsewhere (Sutton, 1979), that a person-centred approach should be the foundation for counselling practice, but that in addition counsellors need a *repertoire* of additional areas of knowledge and skill upon which to draw. This is still my view.

How can we measure the usefulness of this repertoire? How can we judge our skills — with a view to improving them? In other words, how can we evaluate our work? We know of the hazards of subjective perception, of experimenter demand — effects, and even of the differential biases of independent evaluators. How then can we proceed? I suggest, *by inviting our clients to be the evaluator(s) of the service received.*

To do this without access to a full-scale research team seems at first sight impossible. However, since the Truax and Carkhuff publication in 1967, a major contribution has been made through the development of the work of Gerald Egan (1975); his model of 'the skilled helper', with its strong theoretical and evaluative base, is very impressive. In the British literature there seem to be few evaluated studies, but two of note are those of Oldfield (1983) and of Hunt (1985). The former gathered data from users of a Counselling Centre in Oxford upon how helpful they had found the counselling offered; the latter sought information from clients of the National Marriage Guidance Council [now renamed Relate: National Marriage Guidance] upon the perceived usefulness of the counselling they had received.

Surely we can go further than this however? Why should we not adopt an approach which, *from the outset*, builds in a simple means of evaluating the helpfulness of the service offered — by the clients themselves? It is this approach which Martin Herbert and I are developing at Leicester, and which I should now like to describe.

A Model of Evaluating Counselling: the Goal-Attainment Approach

Our thinking developed in this way. I am researching with Martin Herbert means of helping parents to cope with very young children, who, at the ages of two and three, are already beyond the control of their parents. Such children are the cause of acute stress to their young and often isolated parents, and many are at risk of child abuse. We have devised a simple questionnaire where parents specify the areas of difficulty which the family is experiencing: sleep problems, aggressiveness, eating difficulties or parents' feelings of acute personal stress.

After an initial contact-making period, my practice is to agree with the parents what precisely will be happening *from their point of view* if, at the end of our period of work together, they think I have been able to help them. Such a goal might be, and often is, 'that David will sleep through the night, from 7.30 pm to 7.30 am, without disturbing his parents'. Another might be 'that Mrs Andrews will feel able to cope with her anxiety and stress'. These goals are written down.

We meet weekly, and as parents implement the suggestions I make — for example, practising daily relaxation — they tell me whether, against a scale which extends from −5, through 0 to +5, they think things have deteriorated, have remained the same or have improved. Our shared aim is to reach +5. Mrs Andrews' view is of course subjective, but it is *her* subjectivity not mine. Sometimes, because self-report *is* so subjective, it is possible to gain a separate view of any change, perhaps from another member of the family.

This is not the place to expand on the research work with parents; what I seek to do here is to draw people's attention to the value of this goal attainment approach and its relevance to evaluating counselling. It has four stages:

(a) Building relationships and preliminary assessment
(b) Negotiating and agreeing goals with the client(s)
(c) Intervention, towards goals agreed with the client(s)
(d) Evaluation, of the extent to which goals have been met

Let us consider each stage in turn:

Building Relationships, and Preliminary Assessment
First of all time and space is given to establishing a relationship based upon the 'therapeutic triad' described above: accurate empathy, non-possessive warm and genuineness. This may take one session but it may well take more, for the building of trust, as we all know, cannot be hurried. During this time, the counsellor may arrive at some preliminary views upon some of the areas of difficulty which the client is experiencing — but these are regarded as provisional. (It should be stressed that here it is assumed that particular features of a client's circumstances, such as psychotic features, will be recognised and dealt with as emergencies by a different route.)

There follow opportunities for exploring the client's circumstances and perceived difficulties. Here the approach of encouraging people to write a pen portrait of themselves and their difficulties — as written by an understanding friend — may help some. Others may need help in pinpointing just what their difficulties are: they may simply know that they feel 'awful' and do not know what to do about this.

Negotiating and Agreeing Goals with the Client(s)
Next, in the light of what has gone before, and following discussion of the most pressing difficulties *as the client perceives them*, a move can be made towards *agreeing the goals of work together and writing these down*. Such goals might read that by the end of our series of meetings: 'Mrs Jones shall feel able to cope with her anxiety' or 'Mr Davies shall be clearer in his mind about the important decision he has to make' or 'that Mr and Mrs Roberts shall have reduced the number of rows they have weekly by 50 per cent'.

We advocate a written agreement, which includes both a preliminary statement about the number of occasions on which counsellor and client intend to meet, as well as clear goals. Negotiating such an agreement has many advantages. It offers a *shared*, if preliminary, understanding of the focus of work together, and its goals; a helpful structure to a series of meetings, which can sometimes otherwise lose direction and clear purpose; and a clarification of what an agency can and cannot offer. (Thus, if it becomes clear that a client is really wanting the counselling centre to find him a job, then this misconception can be gently corrected.) Finally and most important, it offers a means of evaluation built in from the very beginning.

In view of the evidence of the usefulness of such contracts (for example, from Rosenhan and Seligman, 1984) I would not now myself try to help someone by counselling without such an agreement, or at least, without agreeing that we were working towards writing such an agreement.

Intervention — Towards Goals Agreed with the Client(s)
This stage may overlap with others, and characteristically features much of what is called 'classical' counselling practice. It may be the time when the recognition of unspoken or unacknowledged feelings, the linking of past events with present difficulties, and the discussion of hitherto taboo subjects will occur. Please do not let it seem that we undervalue or disparage these crucial features of the counselling process. We do not. They are central and of the greatest importance. Sometimes the relief of sharing strong or unacknowledged feelings may of itself markedly reduce the misery or hopelessness with which people come. Sometimes there may be minimal relief because the difficulties have no solution.

In addition, however, it is at this stage that the repertoire of knowledge and skill which the counsellor possesses is vital.

We need every morsel of information and skill we can get: knowledge of practical resources from statutory and voluntary agencies; knowledge of organisations offering specialist skills, such as alcohol advice centres; knowledge of how people may pursue their welfare rights entitlement, skills of teaching relaxation and anxiety management — we need all these and more.

For people do not come to counselling centres with neatly packaged difficulties responsive only to internal reflection and the gaining of insight. They come with personal tragedies overlaid with financial problems, with relationship difficulties exacerbated by disadvantages of housing and environment, and with private miseries compounded by mental and physical illness.

Thus it is at this stage that, if appropriate, possible courses of *action* can be discussed: the approach to a relevant agency to seek particular forms of help; the practising of relaxation; or the implementation of any of the particular forms of therapy in which the counsellor may have been trained, and which, to the best of their considered judgement and knowledge of the research, would be helpful to the client(s) concerned.

At every session in this stage, however, it is our practice to invite people to indicate on the −5 to +5 scale which I described above, how they feel they are progressing towards the agreed goals. This can often be very salutary. What I perceive as 'progress' is not always felt to be so by the client. While sometimes my own feelings of pessimism are contradicted by the client's reporting a renewed feeling of confidence and of being able to cope. Progress or lack of progress over the weeks for each goal can be displayed in a simple graph of the type shown in Figure 5.1.

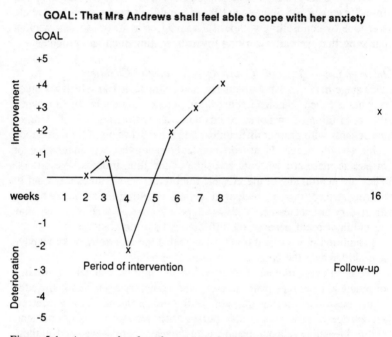

Figure 5.1   *An example of goal-setting and evaluation by the client*

The Stage of Evaluation — of the Extent
to Which Goals have been Achieved

As the agreed number of meetings draws to an end, it will become apparent from the weekly feedback offered by the client whether or not the agreed goals are being, or have been, met. Where they have, this is the time for rejoicing and a shared feeling of satisfaction. Where they have not, then reappraisal is necessary. Questions to be considered will include:

— Would a further series of meeting be profitable?
— Have other matters emerged during counselling which the client did not feel able to disclose earlier, but which clearly need time and consideration?

— Would a specialist agency be able to offer further help?
— Would a change to a different counsellor be helpful?

If the answers to the above questions are Yes, then it is a fairly straightforward matter to negotiate a fresh agreement and to begin a further series of meetings with new or additional goals, or to arrange a referral to another counsellor or another agency. If the answers are No, and the evidence is that many of the original goals have been attained, then counsellor and client may say 'goodbye' — but with a clear understanding that a follow-up meeting at say, two or three months, will be arranged to see whether progress has been maintained. Such a follow-up meeting has many advantages and should be an integral part of the overall service provided.

Adapting the Goal-Attainment Model to any Theory of Counselling

I hope it will be apparent from the above that using a model in which goals are negotiated at the outset in no way precludes the use of any particular theory of counselling or therapy. During the stage of intervention any theory at all which a counsellor feels is ethically appropriate to the needs of the client may be employed. *But it is employed in such a way that its helpfulness can be evaluated.*

In the intervention period then one might see counsellors employing not only ideas from person-centred therapy or principles of transactional analysis, rational-emotive therapy, Gestalt and behaviour therapy — but also engaged in the practicalities of giving information and putting people in touch with services. The goal-attainment approach is not yet another theory of counselling, it *is* a way of structuring intervention, and then of evaluating it.

The approach lends itself well to many of the difficulties brought to counsellors: stress-related problems, relationship worries, low self-esteem, periods of depression, family unhappiness and interpersonal tensions. It can be adapted to work with couples, groups or family systems, although clearly negotiating agreements and contracts with more than one person is a complex task, calling for specialised skills (Herbert, 1981). The approach is somewhat less appropriate and easy to adapt to people with severe illnesses, such as schizophrenia — although I anticipate that in such situations too, the clarification of goals would be found helpful.

In the views of Martin Herbert and myself, its advantages however, are clear: first, it is *ethical*, in that it engages the client(s) from the outset in clarifying expectations and negotiating agreements; second, *if offers a structure* so that both counsellor and client have a framework within which their discussions may take place; third, it allows *evaluation by the client*, the person who has come for help, and who will know far better than the counsellor or any outside observer, whether he or she has found it.

References

Egan, G. (1975) *The skilled helper: a model for systematic helping and interpersonal relating*. Monterey, CA: Brooks/Cole.

Herbert, M. (1981) *Behavioural treatment of problem children: a practice manual*. London: Academic Press.

Hunt, P. (1985) *Clients' responses to marriage counselling: a report on the research project on the follow-up of marriage guidance clients*. (Research Report No. 3). Rugby, Warwicks: National Marriage Guidance Council.

Oldfield, S. (1983) *The counselling relationship*. London: Routledge and Kegan Paul.

Patterson, C. (1977) 'New approaches in counselling: healthy diversity or anti-therapeutic?', *British Journal of Guidance and Counselling*, 5(1): 19–25.

Rachman, S.J. and Wilson, G.T. (1980) *The effects of psychological therapy* (2nd ed.). Oxford: Pergamon.

Rosenhan, D. and Seligman, M. (1984) *Abnormal psychology*. New York: W. W. Norton.

Sutton, C. (1979) *Psychology for counsellors and social workers*. London: Routledge and Kegan Paul.

Truax, R. and Carkhuff, C. (1967) *Towards effective counseling and psychotherapy*. Chicago: Aldine.

Discussion Issues

1   What do *you* consider to be the advantages and disadvantages of helping your clients to specify their outcome goals (See Chapter 1 for an additional discussion of the issue of goals in counselling).

2   To what extent does your preferred approach to counselling recommend that you help your clients specify their outcome goals? If it does so recommend, when does it suggest that you best do this?

3   Under what conditions might you go counter to your preferred approach on these issues?

4   How do you currently attempt to evaluate the outcome of your counselling work with clients?

5   What do *you* consider to be the advantages and disadvantages of using the evaluation approach, outlined by Sutton, in your own counselling practice?

6 Improving the Counseling Relationship

David E. Hutchins

Overview

The TFA System is a practical method counselors can use to adapt theories, techniques, and their personal style to working relationships with clients.

As a counselor, are there times when you feel really good about your working relationship with certain clients? Are there other times when the relationship just does not feel right? One of the reasons for this discrepancy may be that your personal interaction style works well with some people but needs to be adjusted to relate effectively to others. To stimulate thinking about ways to improve the counselor–client relationship, I will propose a method linking counseling theory and techniques to current eclectic practices in counseling and psychotherapy, and I will present practical ways of describing counselor and client behavior. Further, I will propose guidelines that enable counselors to intentionally integrate theory and techniques with each client's behavior so as to increase the probability of establishing an effective working relationship. The thesis of this article is that counselors should base their choice of theories and techniques on each client's behavior.

Experience and Expertise

The above thesis is supported by two major factors that account for the success of many counselors. The first factor is that counselor expertise is enhanced by experience. Distillation of research suggests two possible reasons for this. From Fiedler's (1950a, b) earliest studies of counseling relationships right on through the summarization of research by Auerbach and Johnson (1977), there has been strong and consistent evidence that indicates higher quality relationships with experienced counselors.

This chapter is reprinted by kind permission of the American Association for Counseling and Development from the *Personnel and Guidance Journal* (1984), 62: 572–5.

Such evidence suggests that these experienced counselors are more likely to *adapt* their personal style of relating to clients than are their less experienced counterparts. This adaptation resulting from experience seems more intuitive than systematic; that is, the specific client behavior is not clearly identified. Therefore, necessary counselor adaptation to the client cannot be made easily. Though experienced counselors may be able to *intuitively adapt* their personal interaction to clients, there are no guidelines on precisely how to do it. If we were able to describe a set of guidelines that synthesize these intuitive actions born of experience, we could teach them to prospective counselors and increase our own awareness of how we adapt to clients.

Experience and Eclecticism

The second factor supporting the thesis is that the use of eclectic techniques seems to be the basis of counseling practice for an increasing majority of experienced practitioners. Cormier and Cormier (1979) indicated growing evidence that counselors use a variety of techniques in actual practice. Egan (1975) suggested that the most effective counselor is one with the greatest repertoire of responses. One study surveying 733 PhD clinical psychologists found that 55 per cent (470) identified themselves as having an eclectic approach to counseling (Garfield and Kurtz, 1976). Nisenholz (1983) listed over 100 different approaches to therapy, and Ivey (1980) suggested that there are almost as many approaches to the counseling process as there are counselors and therapists. Finally, Ellis (1982) believed that all counseling and psychotherapy is becoming increasingly eclectic. Such data suggest that a single theoretical approach to working with clients is very probably an inadequate basis for many counseling practitioners.

I believe that increasing eclecticism indicates the counselor's attempt to adapt theory and techniques to each client. Although advocates of major cognitive, affective, and behavioral approaches implicitly suggest that their approach is applicable to everyone, no single theory to date seems adequate for all people. Therefore, the counselor is forced to fashion an appropriate combination of theories and techniques to try and 'fit' each client. Furthermore, though most advocates of particular approaches stress the need for counselors to adapt to client differences, they don't indicate how to adapt to any particular individual. It's almost like saying, 'Here's a theory of counseling . . . but the theory has to be changed to make it work.'

If one considers the broad range of individual differences likely between any two persons, major counselor adjustment in the relationship is probable. A lack of guidelines on how to adapt theories and techniques to an individual client can result in a 'shotgun' kind of experimentation, especially with relatively new counselors. This experimentation results in a counseling version of Russian roulette. Because there are no professional guidelines for when to use what techniques with which clients, the techniques an individual counselor learns from experience remain private knowledge.

In summary, counseling and psychotherapy today have grown beyond the traditional approaches to the extent that the effective practitioner needs to systematically adapt and integrate appropriate elements of theory and techniques into each unique relationship. Because counselor experience is a decided advantage and parts of many different counseling approaches are widely used in practice, practitioners need to ask, 'What combinations of theories and techniques offer the best likelihood of promoting an effective working relationship between the counselor and client?'

Classifying Behavior as Thinking, Feeling, and Acting

I have earlier (Hutchins, 1979, 1982) proposed classifying theories of counseling and psychotherapy into three major categories: thinking, feeling, and acting (TFA). In responding to these articles, Ellis (1982) acknowledged that most counseling theories can be classified into one of these categories. In the TFA System behavior includes how one thinks, feels, and acts. 'Thinking refers primarily to intellectual or cognitive aspects of behavior; feeling refers to emotions or affective aspects; and acting refers to doing something or engaging in activities usually related to one's goals' (Hutchins, 1982: 427). Although there is some overlap in these categories, the TFA System provides a useful way of looking at theories, techniques, behavior patterns, and interaction between people. The goal of TFA is to categorize and synthesize major patterns of behavior, not to 'pigeon hole' people.

In the TFA System the *interaction* between thinking, feeling and acting is important. Do thoughts, feelings, and actions tend to be congruent or discrete and discordant? In what ways? The counselor gathers data on client behavior in the interview by carefully attending to what they talk about, how they talk, and what they do.

The following section will briefly outline behavior typical of people with a predominant orientation in each TFA category. TFA orientations for counselors are also presented. While reading these sketches, think of people who tend to fit into the categories as well as what you are like and how you work as a counselor.

Thinking Orientation

Generally, thinking persons are characterized by intellectual, cognitively oriented behavior. They tend to behave in logical, rational, deliberate, and systematic ways. They are fascinated by the world of concepts, ideas, theories, words, and analytic relationships. The range of behavior in this category runs from minimal thought to considerable depth in quality and quantity of thinking. Organization of thoughts ranges from scattered to highly logical and rational.

Counselors with this orientation tend to focus on what clients think and the consequences. Special attention is paid to what the client says or does not say. Frequently, illogical, irrational thinking is seen as a major cause of client problems. A primary goal of this approach is to change irrational thinking, thus enabling the client to see things more rationally and to resolve problems. Counselors who use this approach are likely to be influenced by the work of Ellis (rational-emotive therapy), Beck (cognitive therapy), Maultsby (rational behavior therapy), and Meichenbaum (cognitive modification).

Feeling Orientation

Feeling persons generally tend to behave in emotionally expressive ways. They are likely to go with their feelings in making decisions: 'If it feels good, do it.' The expression and display of emotions, feelings, and affect provide clues to people with a primary feeling orientation. A person's mood can range from angry, anxious, bitter, hostile, or depressed to one of elation, joy, or enthusiasm. One's emotional energy level can vary from low to high.

Counselors with this orientation are likely to be regarded as especially caring persons. They tend to focus on the client's feelings, paying special attention to how the person talks. Knotted and tangled emotions are seen as a major source of the client's problems. These counselors help the client describe, clarify, and understand mixed up and immobilizing emotions. As emotional incongruencies are straightened out, the client is frequently able to perceive things more clearly (insight). Counselors using this approach are likely to be influenced by the work of Rogers (non-directive, client-centered, person-centered therapy), Perls (Gestalt therapy), Maslow, and a host of phenomenological, humanistic, and existential writers.

Acting Orientation

Acting persons are generally characterized by their involvement in doing things and their strong goal orientation. They are frequently involved with others, and tend to plunge into the thick of things. Action types get the job done, one way or another. To them doing something is better than doing nothing; thus, they are frequently involved in a variety of activities. Their behavior may range from loud, aggressive, and public-oriented to quiet, subtle, and private.

Counselors with an action orientation tend to see client problems as arising from inappropriate actions or a lack of action. These counselors focus particularly on what the client does or does not do, and they tend to encourage clients to begin programs designed to eliminate, modify, or teach new behavior. An action-oriented counselor is likely to be influenced by the work of Bandura (behavior modification), Wolpe (behavior therapy), Krumboltz and Thoresen (behavioral counseling), and others espousing a behavioral approach to change.

TFA Balance

Some people have a more balanced orientation using all three TFA elements. This brief outline of thinking, feeling, and acting modes has exaggerated each to accentuate differences. While some counselors may demonstrate a relative balance in TFA behavior, others tend to express themselves in a more dominant thinking, feeling, or acting mode. A preference for one or more TFA elements tends to be expressed both in counselors' typical interaction with people in general and in their theoretical and practical approach as they interact with clients.

This section has examined three major TFA orientations and the corresponding theoretical approaches used by many counselors. The next section will propose specific suggestions for shifting the counselor's TFA emphasis to enhance the initial relationship and the continuing working relationship with individual clients.

The Counselor–Client Relationship

Two methods will be used here to help in examining the counselor–client relationship in a methodical manner. First, numerical values will be assigned to an individual's behavior pattern by ranking each TFA element as follows: most probable = 3, moderately probable = 2, and least probable = 1. Thus, if one's behavior pattern were F/3, T/2, A/1, the person would be most likely to express feelings and emotions about things (F/3), would be moderately likely to think things through (T/2), and would be least likely to take action (A/1).

Second, the TFA orientation (the styles of the counselor and client) will be compared and contrasted. This will assist in understanding contrasts that explain why some relationships are better or worse than others. The three brief illustrations of counselors with different approaches that follow demonstrate (a) how the counselor's natural relationship with people can lead to client resistance and a poor relationship and (b) how deliberate counselor adaptation to a client's uniqueness can increase the probability of a more effective relationship.

Cognitively Oriented (Thinking) Counselor

Figure 6.1 illustrates TFA patterns of a counselor (T/3, A/2, F/1) and client (F/3, A/2, T/1). The probabilities of behavior occurring are indicated by the varying size of the circles and the number with each TFA element; the larger the circle and number, the greater the probability. In Figure 6.1 the counselor's natural or most characteristic tendency is to interact with

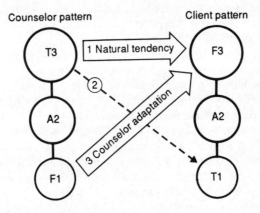

Figure 6.1   *Thinking counselor and feeling client*

people in a highly cognitive manner (T/3). The client, however, is a very feeling, emotionally expressive person (F/3). The counselor's thinking orientation (T/3) in most natural interactions is the least likely behavior mode of the client (T/1) and is therefore likely to generate some resistance. This type of counselor is more likely to enhance the working relationship by first acknowledging the client's feeling orientation (F/3). Adequate recognition of client feelings is likely to increase the client's perception that 'here is a counselor who really understands me.'

If the client's feelings are not dealt with adequately, he or she may be turned off by this cognitively oriented (rational, logical) therapeutic type of approach. By first acknowledging feelings, however, the counselor is more likely to experience success in helping the client change the desired behavior.

Affectively Oriented (Feeling) Counselor
Figure 6.2 shows a counselor (F/3, T/2, A/1) whose natural tendency is to interact with people in a manner that emphasizes the emotional aspects (F/3) of situations. The client (A/3, T/2, F/1) has a strong action orientation (A/3). The counselor, if not ready to adapt to the client's behavior to some degree, is likely to alienate the client. The feeling-oriented counselor (F/3) who does not shift toward the client's action orientation tends to appeal to the least likely behavior mode of the client (F/1).

The clearest illustration of this conflict is a client- or person-centered counselor and an action-oriented client. A feeling focus with an action-type client is likely to frustrate the client, for example, 'The counselor doesn't get down to business and give me anything I can do that makes a difference....All this feeling stuff is a waste...I've got better things to do with my time.' Clearly, the counselor needs to recognize the client's

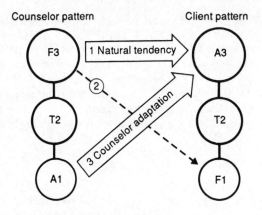

Figure 6.2 *Feeling counselor and acting client*

action orientation and shift this relationship to demonstrate that counseling (and this relationship) has the potential of helping.

Action Oriented (Acting) Counselor
A third example can be seen in Figure 6.3, where the counselor's pattern is A/3, F/2, T/1 and the client's is T/3, F/2, A/1. This counselor is highly action oriented (A/3) in interacting with people, and frequently suggests specific kinds of things the client can do. The client's strongest mode, however, is thinking (T/3). Because this client is least likely to take direct action (A/1), the counselor's action approach is not likely to promote a good working relationship. Such a client would be more likely to first think things through (T/3), then feel good about things (F/2), and finally take action to resolve the situation (A/1).

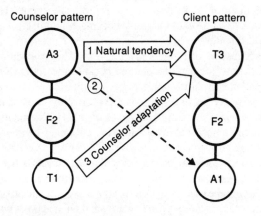

Figure 6.3 *Acting counselor and thinking client*

An illustration of the above could be an instance in which a strongly action oriented counselor (A/3) tries to push the client to take action before the client is intellectually (T/3) and emotionally ready to do so (F/2). The counselor is likely to meet resistance. Such a counselor is more likely to be effective if the client's thoughts are explored (T/3) and the client feels comfortable about them (F/2). Then, the counselor might encourage the client to take action. There is a minimal chance of getting the person to do anything until he or she is able to think through the situation and see things clearly.

Discussion

A counselor's expertise tends to be enhanced by experience, and this experience leads to an increase in the use of eclectic techniques in counseling practice. Research illustrates that increased experience leads to increased counselor adaptability to client behaviors.

Strupp (1977) stated that, 'The art of psychotherapy may largely consist of judicious and sensitive applications of given technique, delicate decisions of when to press a point or when to be patient, when to be warm and understanding or when to be remote' (p. 11). In my opinion evidence indicates that the 'art' of psychotherapy and counseling comes mainly from experience, by means of which counselors intuitively synthesize elements of theory and techniques and adapt their personal relationship to the uniqueness of each client. Thus, each counselor or therapist grows in intuitive personal knowledge with each additional client. Unfortunately there is no gain in specific awareness of how to synthesize appropriate elements for the profession as a whole. Therefore, I have proposed a synthesis of (a) major personal behavior orientations (TFA) of clients and counselors; (b) corresponding theories and techniques; and (c) a specific method of deliberate counselor adaptation to each client. These three elements combine to promote a good working relationship between the counselor and client.

Deliberate counselor adjustment to the client's TFA orientation amounts to being truly client- or person-centered because the counselor adapts to meet each person 'on their own ground.' If the client believes that the counselor understands his or her personal concerns, the client is more likely to believe that counseling can help. As Cousins (1979) suggested, one's belief system can be critical in deciding the outcomes of many different situations.

Throughout the counseling process the counselor adapts behavior in light of each client's orientation. For example, a client with a strong feeling orientation may need to take specific action, but the counselor suggests this action in a manner the client is likely to understand, feel good about, and complete. Thus, the TFA System involves more than matching the client's style.

By implication, two propositions emerge. First, the counselor with the greatest TFA adaptability should be able to work most effectively with the greatest range of clients and concerns. Second, if the counselor cannot adapt appropriately, the range of clients, kinds of problems, and counselor's work setting may be limited, and more clients may need to be referred to others in order to achieve counseling goals.

By adapting to the client's TFA orientation, building on the client's TFA strengths, and integrating TFA strategies, the counselor increases the probability of the client making needed changes in behavior. Extensive testing is underway on an instrument to classify individual TFA orientations. For the time being counselors can improve their interaction with clients by sharpening their observation of thinking, feeling, and acting behavior in the interview setting and by paying close attention to what is said, how it is said, and what the client does or does not do.

It is apparent that to some degree effective counselors base their choice of theories and techniques on the behavior of each client. As a profession we have grown beyond the point where a single approach to counseling and psychotherapy is appropriate — if it ever was. Now it is essential to address the most critical task in counseling by answering such questions as: What works? For which clients? With which concerns? A synthesis of client and counselor behavior, a variety of counseling theories and techniques, and a specific method of adapting these elements to an individual client should help provide answers to these questions.

References

Auerbach, A. and Johnson, M. (1977) 'Research on the therapist's level of experience' in A. Gurman and A. Razin (eds), *Effective psychotherapy* (pp. 84–102). Elmsford, NY: Pergamon Press.

Cormier, W.H. and Cormier, L.S. (1979) *Interviewing strategies for helpers: a guide to assessment, treatment, and evaluation.* Monterey, CA: Brooks/Cole.

Cousins, N. (1979) *Anatomy of an illness as perceived by the patient.* New York: W.W. Norton.

Egan, G. (1975) *The skilled helper: a model for systematic helping and interpersonal relating.* Monterey, CA: Brooks/Cole.

Ellis, A. (1982) 'Major systems', *Personnel and Guidance Journal*, 61: 6–7.

Fiedler, F.E. (1950a) 'Factor analyses of psychoanalytic, nondirective, and Adlerian therapeutic relationships', *American Psychologist*, 5: 324–5.

Fiedler, F.E. (1950b) 'The concept of an ideal therapeutic relationship', *Journal of Consulting Psychology*, 14: 239–45.

Garfield, S.L. and Kurtz, R. (1976) 'Clinical psychologists in the 1970s', *American Psychologist*, 31: 1–9.

Hutchins, D.E. (1979) 'Systematic counseling: the T–F–A model for counselor intervention', *Personnel and Guidance Journal*, 57: 529–31.

Hutchins, D.E. (1982) 'Ranking major counseling strategies with the TFA/Matrix system', *Personnel and Guidance Journal*, 60: 427–31.

Ivey, A.E., with Simek-Downing, L. (1980) *Counseling and psychotherapy: Skills, theories, and practice*. Englewood Cliffs, NJ: Prentice-Hall.

Nisenholz, B. (1983) 'Solving the psychotherapy glut', *Personnel and Guidance Journal*, 61: 535–6.

Strupp, H. (1977) 'A reformulation of the dynamics of the therapist's contribution', in A. Gurman and A. Razin (eds), *Effective psychotherapy* (pp. 1–22). Elmsford, NY: Pergamon Press.

Discussion Issues

1   Using Hutchins' TFA framework, what is your own dominant *counselling* pattern?

2   To what extent is this congruent with your own *personal* TFA pattern? How have you dealt with any discrepancies between the two?

3   How might *you* use the TFA framework to accommodate to your clients' TFA patterns?

4   What difficulties might you experience in accommodating to different client TFA patterns? How might you overcome any such difficulties?

5   At present, how do you vary your own counselling approach to accommodate to differences between clients? What are the salient factors that influence you to vary your counselling behaviour in this way?

7 The Stages of Influence in Counseling

Terence J. Tracey

Viewing counseling as an influence process is becoming much more common, as is evidenced by recent research in the area. Much of the research has focused on how the counselor influences the client. The assumption being that if we know how the counselor influences the client, then we can influence our clients more effectively. However, this approach neglects the effect or influence the client has on the counselor. Although much recognition is given to the concept of mutual influence, little research and conceptualization has been done from this perspective. If the concept of mutual influence is valid, then it would be expected that the influence attempts of each of the participants would vary over time, reflecting the cumulative effect that each person had on the other. In this view, the influence of either participant is not a static trait. Examination of the influence process thus requires a study of how each person attempts to influence the other over time. The purpose of this chapter is to present a stage model of successful counseling that focuses on how the client and counselor attempt to influence each other over the course of treatment.

The goal of treatment in this model is to enable the client to be effective in his or her influence attempts. It is assumed that all individuals attempt to influence their environment, that is other people, to meet their needs. Clients seek help because they are not as successful as they would like to be in getting their needs met. The task of the counselor is to help the client gain more appropriate means of influencing others to better meet his or her needs. The manner of achieving this task requires that the counselor first recognize how the client attempts to influence his or her environment and then work to get the client to try new means of influence that would be more realistic and effective. The accomplishment of this change in client influence attempts is hypothesized to be associated with three relatively distinct stages of the counseling interaction. Each stage represents a different influence strategy that the counselor uses in response to client influence attempts. It is proposed that all three stages are necessary

This chapter is reprinted (with slight modification) by kind permission of Charles C. Thomas, Publisher, from *The Social Influence Process in Counseling and Psychotherapy* (1984) (ed. F.J. Dorn).

for successful outcome. Partial movement through the three stages is associated with less successful outcome.

Early Stage

The first stage relates to establishing rapport with the client, which implies that the goal of this stage is for the client to feel understood and valued. The attainment of rapport is proposed to be a function of the extent to which the counselor acts in a manner in line with the client's influence attempts. All clients enter counseling with certain expectations regarding what is to occur, for example what each person is to do, what are appropriate foci, and how topics should be discussed. These expectations are both conscious and unconscious, and the client attempts to influence the counselor into acting according to them in both explicit and subtle ways. Implied in these expectations are certain preferred behaviors from the counselor which the client attempts to elicit (Beier, 1966; Kell and Mueller, 1966). If the counselor behaves according to these expectations, the client should feel understood and valued, because the counselor is following the client's definition of what should occur. The less the counselor adheres to the client's expectations and influence attempts, the less the client will feel understood and valued. Successful traversing of this initial stage of rapport attainment is dependent upon the counselor (a) accurately perceiving the relationship expectations of the client, both realistic and unrealistic, and (b) acting according to them.

An example of poor negotiation of the rapport stage would be the client who enters counseling strongly expressing a desire to keep things on an intellectual level, yet who is also expressing, albeit much less clearly, particular areas of pain and a desire for comfort. The client will be attempting to get the counselor to act both on an overt intellectual and a covert emotional level. The extent to which the counselor can act according to both, somewhat conflicting and unrealistic client influence attempts, will be the extent to which the client will feel understood. If the counselor responds to only one of the influence attempts (for example overt discussion of pain), the client will not feel completely understood.

If the counselor does not do an adequate job of recognizing and meeting client expectations, it could be expected that the client would terminate prematurely (Lennard and Bernstein, 1967), as his or her needs were not met. Thus, successful movement through this early, rapport stage is a function of the extent to which the counselor is able to accept the client's 'neurotic' relationship definition and influence attempts.

Middle Stage

If the initial rapport building stage has been successfully managed, what exists is a relationship determined relatively exclusively by the client. By accepting the client's definition of the relationship, the counselor has reinforced the client's unrealistic definition of the relationship. It is assumed that these unrealistic, 'neurotic' relationship expectations and associated realtionship influence attempts are the client's problem. The client has defined the relationship in a manner that reduces client anxiety by not allowing the counselor to have any input. The middle stage is characterized by the counselor changing tactics and not acting so much according to client relationship definition.

This alteration of counselor behavior results in a conflict over who is to influence what will occur. Each participant is trying to define the relationship and influence the other based on his or her own definitions while not accepting the definitions of the other. As the counselor starts to try and relate to the client in more realistic ways, for example by being more direct about some of the earlier implicit messages, the client becomes more anxious and feels less understood. The client wishes to return to the old, comfortable relationship and attempts to influence the counselor to act accordingly. To influence the counselor to go back to earlier ways of acting, the client will resort to very powerful and unrealistic influence ploys; an extreme example of which would be to threaten suicide. The counselor in this middle stage should resist acting completely according to client unrealistic expectations and influence attempts. What results in each person resisting, to some extent, what the other wants. The client desires a re-establishment of the initial unrealistic 'neurotic' relationship, where he or she felt very comfortable, and the counselor is attempting to get the client to relate in a realistic, give-and-take, mutually determined manner.

It is this conflict stage that results in change in the client. The more the counselor does not act according to the client's definition, the more the client will increase his or her influence attempts to bring the relationship back to where it was. The counselor will resist these influence attempts. This continued counselor resistance to the client's attempts to return the relationship to the earlier position will stimulate client change. With time, the client will be forced to start adopting more realistic views of the relationship, or at least be more open to mutual definition. This openness to mutual relationship definition is indicative of more healthy functioning. This change process can be explained by viewing the counselor's behavior as not reinforcing the client's unrealistic influence attempts. Given this lack of reinforcement and a probable prior history of intermittent reinforcement, it would be expected that the client would increase unrealistic influence attempts to obtain reinforcement. Then, as little further reinforcement would be forthcoming, the client would start using new behaviors that would be more likely to be reinforced by others (Beier, 1966).

Successful movement through this middle, conflict stage is dependent upon the counselor skillfully maintaining a balance between conforming to (support) and acting different from (conflict) the client's unrealistic expectations.

If the counselor acts according to the client's definition, that is, the counselor introduces little new behavior, the relationship will be viewed by both participants as fairly comfortable. No change will occur. Conversely, too much conflict, caused by the counselor acting very differently from the initial agreed relationship definition, can result in premature termination. It is assumed that what keeps the client in treatment is the hope of returning to the earlier, comfortable relationship where one's needs were met, albeit unrealistically. If the current counseling relationship is too discrepant from the earlier one, it would be harder for clients to sustain this hope and easier just to give up by withdrawing. The amount of conflict introduced by the counselor in this middle stage must be constantly monitored.

This optimal amount of conflict and its timing (abruptness versus gradualness) is hypothesized to be related to the disturbance level of the client. The healthy client can endure more conflict and, as such, much more therapist deviation from expectation is possible. Movement into the middle, conflict stage could thus be much more abrupt, given the client's resources. However, more disturbed clients would require much more support and could endure much less conflict. Movement into the middle stage would have to be slow and gradual, with the counselor deviating only slightly from the original expectations. Thus, treatment would be much longer. For the more disturbed client, too high a conflict/support ratio can result in withdrawal (either physically or psychologically), while the exact same conflict/support ratio may not be enough to affect change in a healthier client. So, successful travel through this middle conflict stage requires the counselor to be able to: (a) assess the optimal conflict/support level that can be used to effect client change, and (b) be flexible enough to vary his or her behavior away from initially agreed behaviors to achieve this optimum balance.

Late Stage

The final-resolution stage comes about as the client starts to develop more realistic relationship definitions. The client becomes less wedded to unrealistic, unilateral definitions of what is to occur in the relationship. He or she begins to notice the counselor as a real person, with his or her own input, for the first time. How each person is to act with the other is openly negotiated for the first time. The initial counseling relationship was based exclusively on the client's definitions. As clients treat the therapeutic realtionship more realistically, they are also approaching outside issues, problems, and relationships equally realistically. Again, there is harmony in the relationship, but, instead of being based exclusively on the client's definition as in the initial stage, it is based on a mutual definition of what is to occur. In this stage, the client experiments with a variety of new behaviors and relationship definitions to get a feel for his or her level of comfort. This is often an exciting yet threatening stage, but the client is dealing with the anxiety openly and is largely amenable to feedback, unlike previously. In this stage, the counselor is more free to act as a real person and to give opinions. But often-times, this is when the counselor is least required, as the client is better able to openly address his or her needs in ways that others, outside treatment, can respond. Much of the reinforcement of new appropriate behavior should occur outside of counseling.

Overall, a three-stage model has been proposed and defined by three different tasks of the counselor. The counselor first behaves in accordance with client influence attempts and relationship definition (rapport stage), then the counselor alters his or her behavior away from the client definition (conflict stage), and, finally, as the client is able to deal realistically with the relationship, the counselor pulls back and initiates termination. The central dimension of this stage model is its focus on the communication between the participants as the vehicle of influence. Specifically, the proposed model is reflected in the relative communicational harmony between the participants. The first and third stages are hypothesized to have relatively harmonious communication, because each participant's actions are understood and agreed upon by the other, even though the initial relationship is client determined and the later relationship is more mutually determined. The middle stage, on the other hand, should demonstrate somewhat less harmonious communication (less agreements, less following of other's topics or desires, more conflict, and more open expression of negative affect) because what each person should do is much less in agreement. With respect to communicational harmony, then, the proposed stage model will evidence a high-low-high pattern over time.

A graph of this proposed model of successful counseling is presented as line A in Figure 7.1. The other lines in Figure 7.1 depict the various ways that counseling could result in a less successful outcome. Line B represents a failure to establish rapport due to the counselor not acting according to client expectations and influence attempts. The client will try harder to get the counselor to understand and to act accordingly, while the counselor will be trying harder to define what is to occur in his or her own way. Communication will not be harmonious, as neither will be acting as the other desires. If continued over time, each will become dissatisfied and most likely the client will fail to return. Line C represents a failure on the counselor's part to move the relationship into the middle conflict stage. The counselor continues to act according to the early client definitions of the relationship and thus each other's actions are not in conflict. No change is introduced in the counselor's behavior, and thus no client change will result. Line D represents what occurs if the counselor introduces too much change in behavior during the middle conflict stage.

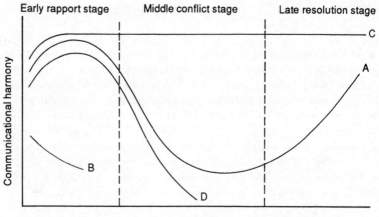

Figure 7.1   *Graphs of the hypothesized pattern of communicational harmony over the course of treatment. Line A represents successful counseling. Lines B through D represent the three types of unsuccessful outcome associated with this model. Line B represents a failure to achieve rapport. Line C represents a failure to enter the conflict stage. Line D represents the introduction of too much conflict.*

This large change in counselor behavior results in an increase in communicational conflict, but the amount of conflict is too much for the client to endure. The promise of returning to the more harmonious early stage appears impossible given the current disharmony, so the client terminates.

   The validity of the proposed stage model has been examined in only a few studies. Dietzel and Abeles (1975) and Tracey and Ray (1984) have found support for the hypothesized high-low-high pattern of communicational harmony in successful counseling, and the flat profile (line C) for the unsuccessful work. Duehn and Proctor (1977) found support for the presence of line B of Figure 7.1. Communicational disharmony (assessed by the extent to which the participants could agree on topics of conversation) was found to be higher in those dyads that terminated prematurely. Overall, there is some support for the validity of the proposed stage model, although much work is needed. But, the hypothesized model also has some interesting implications regarding client-counselor matching.

Client–Counselor Matching

Given the importance of the counselor acting according to the client's relationship definition in the early stage, it makes sense to assign clients to counselors who would be more likely to match their expectations. For example, counselors vary greatly on the extent to which they are able or desire to structure the interaction. Those clients who expect a directive counselor would probably feel more comfortable and understood with a counselor who manifested these directive and structuring behaviors. In principle, matching clients with counselors who have a greater likelihood of behaving according to client expectations would lead to quicker rapport and fewer premature terminations.

The key to client assignment would thus be the relative similarity of client expectations to the behavior repertoire of the counselor. If this discrepancy were great, it would be presumed to be more difficult to establish rapport. Conversely, given great similarity of client expectations and counselor behavior, it would be very easy to establish a quick and strong rapport. But the research examining this hypothesis has yielded equivocal results (Duckro, Beal and George, 1979).

There are three major problems with the matching concept. The first and most glaring is measurement of client expectations, especially some of the unrealistic and covertly expressed ones. With more disturbed clients, this assessment would be especially difficult because a greater proportion would be covert and conflicting. Given the subtle nature of these expectations it is hard to assume that paper-and-pencil measures would be able to reflect the entire domain, although this may be a start. Perhaps the best means of assessing these dimensions appears to be an assessment of the client by a particularly skilled counselor(s) who would be sensitive to these subtle role expectations. This type of diagnostic assessment is what has been called for by McLemore and Benjamin (1979).

Even given excellent measurement of the client's role expectations, the issue of counselor skill is paramount. Some counselors are flexible enough in behavior that, although they may prefer one type of behavior in counseling, they are able to adapt to a wide variety of client expectations. Other counselors are skilled in establishing rapport with only those clients whose expectations fit the style they prefer. It seems plausible to propose that client-counselor matching will yield three distinct groupings: (1) those with an excellent match which will almost certainly result in a well-established rapport, (2) those with a moderate mismatch of client expectations with counselor preferred behavior which would result in unclear rapport, and (3) those of great mismatch where it would be almost impossible to establish rapport. It seems obvious that if the client's expectations match well with the counselor's preferred behavior, that rapport would come easy. Similarly, if the client expected the counselor to act in a manner extremely different from the counselor's preference ability, it would be extremely difficult to establish rapport. The grouping where counselor skill is expected to make the most impact is the middle group of moderate discrepancy. Skilled counselors would be those who could adapt their behavior somewhat to meet the expectations of the client. Less skilled counselors would be those who would have more trouble altering their behavior or style. Although all counselors could be very effective in helping their clients, as defined here a skilled counselor would be one who is more flexible in counseling style and thus would be able to establish rapport with a greater range of clients.

The other drawback to matching is that even if the client and counselor were perfectly matched, there is no guarantee that the matched dyads would result in better outcome. Matching is only hypothesized to be related to attainment of initial rapport, not movement through the conflict or resolution stages. In fact, it may be expected that a perfect match of client expectations and counselor-preferred behavior may be detrimental to a successful outcome. Given a good match, it may be harder for the counselor to alter his or her behavior in the middle stage so as to stimulate client change. If the counselor is quite comfortable in the initial role, it would be presumably more difficult for him or her to change behavior, as changing would feel inappropriate to the counselor. A common example of this is the counselor's encouragement of client dependence in the middle stages rather than the counselor attempting to stimulate independence.

Conclusions and Implications

The model proposed here involves viewing counseling as a process whereby each participant is attempting to influence the other. Successful outcome is proposed to be a function of the counselor skillfully adopting three relatively separate influence strategies over the course of treatment. Poor use of counselor influence is proposed to be related to less or unsuccessful outcome. The proposed model has implications for practice, research, and training.

The stage model presents the counselor with a relatively easily monitored means of assessing one's progress in treatment. If the counselor realizes that rapport is hard to establish, he or she may start looking for the subtle and conflicting expectations and influence attempts that had been overlooked. Similarly, if the counselor notices that the dyad has not moved into the conflict stage, he or she would start to look for ways that this could be accomplished. Obviously, more validation of the model is required, but it does provide some cues as to altering counselor behavior to effect change.

The proposed stage model implies that reseachers should look for differences in client and counselor influence over the entire course of treatment. If the model is valid, studies that examine only a few sessions of actual counseling would yield only very partial results which could not at all be said to be representative of what occurs in treatment. Also, given the great variability in rates of movement through the different stages, it makes little sense to aggregate process data across dyads by session numbers. One dyad could be engaged in the conflict stage in session two while another dyad is just starting to establish rapport. Aggregating these two dyads to represent early counseling would not be valid in either case.

Finally, as depicted in this model, the successful counselor is required to have three skills: (a) the ability to recognize the realistic and unrealistic expectations of the client, be they clearly or implicitly expressed, (b) an ability to alter his or her own behavior to meet these client expectations, and (c) an ability to know the right amount of behavior change to introduce for stimulating change, yet not overwhelming the client. These skills require counselor perceptiveness (to recognize subtle and conflicting client expectations) and flexibility (to change behavior according to need). In this model the counselor is expected to engage in three separate types of influence behaviors at different points in the treatment process. Counselors with very strong behavior preferences or with a restricted behavioral repertoire will be at a disadvantage, as they will only be able to treat successfully a smaller range of clients and/or they will have difficulty in making the transitions between stages. An ability to act in a variety of ways in response to any stimulus is key to skillful practice, and we should make attempts to expand our trainee's behavioral repertoire.

References

Beier, E.G. (1966) *The silent language of psychotherapy*. Chicago: Aldine.

Dietzel, C.S. and Abeles, N. (1975) 'Client-therapist complementarity and therapeutic outcome', *Journal of Counseling Psychology*, 24: 399–405.

Duckro, P., Beal, D. and George, C. (1979) 'Research on the effects of disconfirmed client role expectations in psychotherapy: a critical review', *Psychological Bulletin*, 86: 260–75.

Duehn, W.D. and Proctor, E.K. (1977) 'Initial client interaction and premature discontinuance in treatment', *American Journal of Orthopsychiatry*, 47: 284–90.

Kell, B.L. and Mueller, W.J. (1966) *Impact and change: a study of counseling relationships*. New York: Appleton-Century-Crofts.

Lennard, H.L. and Bernstein, A. (1967) 'Role learning in psychotherapy', *Psychotherapy: Theory, Research and Practice*, 4: 1–6.

McLemore, C.W. and Benjamin, L.S. (1979) 'Whatever happened to interpersonal diagnosis?: a psychosocial alternative to DSM-III', *American Psychologist*, 34: 17–34.

Tracey, T.J. and Ray, P.B. (1984) 'Stages of successful time-limited counseling: an interactional examination', *Journal of Counseling Psychology*, 31: 13–27.

Discussion Issues

1 To what extent do you agree with Tracey that counsellors and clients are engaged in a process of mutual influence in counselling?

2 Do you attempt to meet your clients' initial 'relationship definition and influence attempts'? If so, why and to what extent? If not, why not?

3 How do you attempt to introduce 'productive' conflict into the middle stage of counselling with your clients? And how do you respond to their attempts to bring the relationship back to where it was in the initial stage?

4 To what extent do you agree with Tracey that when the client is able to deal realistically with his or her relationship with the counsellor, the latter should pull back and initiate the termination process?

5 Looking at your typical counselling behaviour during the early, middle and late stages of the counselling process, can you identify ways in which your behaviour reliably varies over time? If so, how do you account for such variation?

8 Transference Phenomena in the Counseling Situation

C. Edward Watkins, Jr

Overview

This article explores the transference phenomenon and some of its manifestations in the counseling situation. Also, methods for managing clients' transference behaviors are proposed.

The counseling experience entails a distinct type of helping relationship characterized by diverse and complex interactions that occur within a unique interpersonal context. Such a relationship includes several identifiable variables, these being: (a) the counselor; (b) the client; (c) the counseling relationship; and (d) the counseling environment. Each of these variables carries or reflects its own particular constellation of constitutional and psychosocial elements. Deriving from this intermingling of elements, the bond between helper and helpee develops, proving effective either facilitatively, neutrally, or deterioratively.

One aspect of the counseling relation–transference actions and reactions is of special significance in the therapeutic situation. These manifestations, typically evidenced by clients who experience the gamut of personal concerns, can have varied effects upon the establishment and maintenance of the counseling relationship. As a result, the managing of the transference is a critical issue that bears heavily upon the outcome of counseling. Failure to deal with transference feelings and expressions can create myriad difficulties in counseling and, as Basch (1980) indicated, is a common reason for unsuccessful treatment efforts. Considering the importance of transference and its potential impact in counseling, this aspect of the therapeutic relationship will be examined subsequently. Specifically, the concept of transference will be explored, some of its manifestations in the counseling situation presented, and a model for understanding such manifestations outlined.

This chapter is reprinted by kind permission of the American Association for Counseling and Development from the *Personnel and Guidance Journal* (1983), 62: 206–10.

Some Considerations on Transference

Transference has been viewed from different vantage points in the counseling and psychotherapy literature. At present, there are two basic perspectives on this phenomenon. First is the broad, all-inclusive (perhaps overinclusive) interpretation that defines transference as any client feeling, thought, or action that occurs in counseling; 'everything . . . is a transference phenomenon' (Bellak and Faithorn, 1981: 131). The problem with this interpretation is its discounting of nontransference, realistically-based behaviors (Greenson, 1971, 1972). Consequently, the counselee cannot win, so to speak. Furthermore, if every client action is to be construed as transference, then it would follow that every counselor action is of a countertransference nature (Kernberg, 1965; Panken, 1981). Thus, neither participant in the relationship interacts with any 'real' here-and-now expressions.

A second view of transference that will be used in this article relates directly to the client's early relationships with significant others, particularly parents. More specifically, transference can be construed as 'the carry-over of childhood interpersonal attitudes toward present-day interpersonal relations' (Fine, 1975: 105). In this sense, it is a 'transferral . . . of sentiments, drives, and conflicts experienced in the past to current situations and people' (Bellak and Faithorn, 1981: 131). Such a transfer can occur in myriad relationships, including teacher, mate, friends, and counselor, among others. Also, it can be manifested in diverse ways, for example, a desire for affection (MacKinnon and Michels, 1971), provision of gifts (Langs, 1973, 1974), varied requests for gratification (Gelso, 1979), and fear of rejection (Adatto, 1977).

In examining further the manifestations of transference, expressions of the client are generally described as either positive or negative in nature; thus, the terms *positive transference* and *negative transference* frequently emerge. Positive transferential reactions include feelings of liking, solicitude, and loving toward the helper. Conversely, negative reactions can involve distrust, disliking, or even hate. Although these concepts prove interesting, many analytic practitioners believe they oversimplify or cloud the complexity of the therapeutic relationship (Arlow, 1979; Colby, 1951; MacKinnon and Michels, 1971). Therefore, some therapists (Reid, 1980) have suggested that transference be considered primarily in light of visible feelings or behavioral manifestations; others have presented innovative conceptualizations of transference as an interactive phenomenon (Langs, 1978, 1980, 1982).

As can be discerned, transference is a multifaceted concept that has been viewed from different vantages. Although these different vantage points merit review, some more concrete means of defining the term also seems needed. One attempt at doing this has been offered by Basch (1980). He described the transference experience as a rather specific expectational set that predisposes the client to perceive and act — react toward situations and people in a somewhat decided way. Consequently, the counselee enters a relationship — be it of an impersonal, friendly, or therapeutic nature — with a fixed bent in perceptions and feelings. This can result in the client's misperceptions of the counselor's personality as well as misperceptions of those efforts advanced by the helper. In essence, the counselee's apperceptive schema can bias and distort reality, and it is such distortions that often prove problematic for the client.

In conceiving of the transference pattern as expectational set, some of the difficulties that accrue to this pattern can be more easily identified. For one, transference is often an attempt to structure and define the present via the past. Stated differently, it is an attempt to maintain the status quo (Paolino, 1981; Singer, 1970). Clients then engage in self-preservative behaviors and forgo opportunities for self-enhancement. Viewed in such a manner, transference represents an ego defensive operation — a psychic displacement of sorts (Laughlin, 1979) — that serves to protect one's self-image. Singer (1970) characterized the concept of transference well, describing it as a 'vehicle for self-elimination' (p. 285) that 'makes for a marked diminution of [the] sense of self' (p. 285). More pointedly, he stated that, 'Transference reactions reduce self-awareness by helping [clients] maintain a world image in which all people are seen in essentially identical terms, thus eliminating differentiated experience. [Transference, then, is a pervasive] leveling process' (p. 289); 'in simplest terms, . . . a "whitewash"' (p. 288).

Considering these effects of transference patterns, it is understandable why the recognition and management of the transference is accorded such importance (Blanck, 1976; Gill, 1979; King, 1980; Neubauer, 1980; Storr, 1980). Thus, attention to this phenomenon would seem of marked significance to most if not all counselors — especially those engaged in the practice of therapeutic counseling and psychotherapy. In the remainder of this article, I will address some means through which transference behaviors are evidenced in the counseling situation.

Transference Patterns in Counseling and Psychotherapy

Although there are conceivably innumerable transference patterns that clients can manifest, five such patterns frequently appear in the work of counseling. These include perceptions of the counselor as: (a) ideal, (b) seer, (c) nurturer, (d) frustrator, and (e) nonentity. Each perceptual pattern, along with some of the varied aspects that attend it, is considered subsequently. The reader may find Table 8.1 to be of value in further clarifying the material presented.

Table 8.1   Conceptualizing and intervening in transference patterns

Transference Pattern	Client Attitudes-Behaviors	Counselor Experience	Intervention Approach
Counselor as ideal	Profuse complimenting, agreements Bragging about counselor to others Imitating counselor's behaviors Wearing similar clothing Hungering for counselor's presence General idealization	Pride, satisfaction, strength Feelings of being all-competent Tension, anxiety, confusion Frustration, anger	Focus on: client's expectations effects of these expectations intra-punitive expressions trend toward self-negation tendency to give up oneself
Counselor as seer	Ascribes omniscience, power to counselor Views counselor as 'the expert' Requests answers, solutions Solicitation of advice	Feelings of being all-knowing Expertness, 'God-complex' Self-doubt, questioning of self Self-disillusionment Sense of incompetence	Focus on: client's need for advice lack of decision lack of self-trust opening up of options
Counselor as nurturer	Profuse emotion, crying Dependence and helplessness Indecision, solicitation of advice Desire for physical touch, to be held Sense of fragility	Feeling of sorrow, sympathy Urge to sooth, coddle, touch Experiences of frustration, ineptitude Depression and despair Depletion	Focus on: client's need for dependence feeling of independence unwillingness to take responsibility for self behavioral-attitudinal alternatives
Counselor as frustrator	Defensive, cautious, guarded Suspicious and distrustful 'Enter-exit' phenomenon Testing of counselor	Uneasiness, on edge, tension 'Walking on eggshells' experience Increased monitoring of responses Withdrawal and unavailability Dislike for client Feelings of hostility, hate	Focus on: trust building relationship enhancement purpose of transference pattern consequences of trusting others reworking of early experience
Counselor as nonenity	'Topic shifting', lack of focus Volubility, thought pressure Desultory, aimless meanderings	Overwhelmed, subdued Taken aback Feelings of being used, discounted Lack of recognition Sense of being a 'nonperson', Feelings of resentment, frustration Experience of uselessness	Focus on: establishing contact getting behind the client's verbal barrier effects of quietness-reflection on client distancing effects of the transference

Counselor as Ideal

In this particular frame, the client regards the counselor as the ideal person. The counselor in essence and effect is considered 'the perfect individual' — someone who does everything just right, without flaw or error. From a psychoanalytic perspective, the helper is attributed an idealized image, perhaps reminiscent of how the client initially viewed one's parents. Should this type of image be ascribed, it becomes blatantly manifest in the client's behaviors, and its manifestations can take a number of varied yet consistent forms. Some of these include: (a) profuse complimenting of the counselor; (b) bragging about the therapist to others; (c) continually agreeing with the counselor's interpretations or reflections; and (d) 'hungering' for the helper's presence or communications. More subtle but noticeable means involve dressing like the counselor, sitting in a similar style, changing sitting positions in concert with the therapist, or using the helper's words, phrases, or structuring of sentences.

Identifying such a pattern, as with the others to follow, can be ascertained via a myriad of channels. Two particular methods, however, seem most fundamental: (a) attention to the counselor–client dialogue (Leavy, 1980); and (b) the counselor's focusing upon inner experience (Friedman, 1970). Through these means, the counselor often is able to distinguish particular forms of transference behavior and their effects. For example, in reference to the client's idealization of the therapist, the helper who is so regarded may initially feel a sense of pride, strength, and competence. There can be a feeling of experiencing doing one's job well and of successfully intervening in the life of another. Such thoughts and feelings can persist for a while, but frequently the 'honeymoon period' (Nacht, 1959) ends as the counselor more clearly recognizes the pattern being manifested. This recognition may come through a shift in feelings toward the client. No longer is the proud, all-competent image maintained; instead, the counselor can feel some measure of tension, anxiety, and confusion with the client that soon gives way to frustration and anger.

Intervening in the idealized pattern requires two fundamental attitudes on the counselor's part: (a) the provision of ongoing ego support to the client; and (b) an ability to tolerate the client's disappointment, depression, and perhaps anger when the transference stance is confronted. In confronting idealization, a focus upon the counselee's expectations seems needed. Along with an examination of how these expectations affect the counselor–client dyad, their influence upon the helpee's intimate and friendly relations can also be considered. Such explorations facilitate the client's recognition and understanding of this transference pattern; consequently, modifications can be adopted and instituted. Although an assessment of interpersonal expectations is warranted, so too is an analysis of the client's intrapsychic 'intrapunitive' expressions. These expressions can involve various forms of self-effacement and self-negation. More specifically, in the counseling session the helpee may give up the self, thus becoming somewhat of a shadow figure or, to use Winnicott's (1975) term, a *false self*. As this aspect emerges, its recognition and resolution can be a critical part of therapy. Consequently, the counselor's sensitivity to and clarification of such a pattern is often quite significant to treatment outcome.

Counselor as Seer
This pattern, which shares some similarities with the previous set, frequently entails ascriptions of omniscience, expertness, and power to the counselor. The helper is regarded as someone who knows all the right answers and is often attributed a superordinate psychological knowledge by the client. From such attributions, the client then may expect advice from the therapist and eagerly anticipate any suggestions cr recommendations that can be provided. In essence, the counselee says, 'tell me; you know what's best.'

Initially, some counselors may fall prey to this transference pattern. They enjoy the feelings of expertness with which they're granted and revel in the experience of power. For a while, a self-intoxication of sorts can occur in which both counselor and client collude in a distorted type of misalliance (Langs, 1973, 1974, 1975). Such self-intoxication wears off, however, leading to the therapist's questioning and doubting of oneself. Should this disillusionment continue, it can result in marked feelings of despair and incompetence — a feeling of being a failure and thereby having failed the client.

To deal effectively with the transference pattern in question, the client's attributions can be used as a focal point. More specifically, the client's ascriptions of power and expertness to the therapist as well as others can be scrutinized. The effects of this set can then be illuminated, along with some of its underlying purposes or motives. Furthermore, the client's need for such a pattern can be considered. By neither trusting oneself nor making one's own decisions, the counselee conveys much useful information regarding one's self-representation and its ultimate implementation. In many of these cases, there may be a deeply ingrained feeling of inferiority and a real fear of self-decision. Thus, through always placing others into a deciding role, the client doesn't experience the possibility of making an incorrect response and, consequently, remains in a protective, preservative stance. Moving clients from this stance toward one of risking, though frequently a difficult task, is essentially the purpose of challenging the 'seer' pattern.

Counselor as Nurturer
Counselees who often view the counselor in this manner act in a helpless, inept fashion. They feel unable to act decisively and, thus, vacillate between

the stances of activity and inactivity. Furthermore, they communicate an appearance of utter fragility that frequently accompanies a marked orientation toward dependency and fusion. Such behaviors can become manifest through numerous channels, including the expression of profuse emotion, crying, and fear, among others. To stave off these intense feelings, the client is prone to solicit, even demand, some sense of strict order from the counselor. Solutions, answers, and decisions are all needed urgently; without these the helpee's confusion and fear escalate, resulting in withdrawal into a 'shell' or womb-like cocoon. Also, as feelings of vulnerability and 'ego-weakness' become increasingly prominent, requests for physical touch, holding, and hugging can be made. In more severe circumstances, a desire for sexual contact — signifying union with the stronger object, the counselor — may be evidenced.

Recognition of this transference pattern often can be witnessed in the counselor's soothing gestures or behaviors toward the client. The helper not only feels an urge to coddle, stroke, and nurse the counselee, but may experience a deep sorrow and sympathy for the client. Should the counselor be unable to recognize such affects, while simultaneously maintaining an appropriate distance from the client, the therapist is apt to become overly mired in a debilitating countertransference reaction. As a result, a pervasive experience of frustration, ineptitude, and depression can ensue. The counselor and client may then engage in a collusive, nongratifying relationship that proves deteriorative in effect.

Catching oneself in this type of interaction, as the Adlerian literature emphasizes (Dinkmeyer, Pew and Dinkmeyer, 1979; Mosak, 1979), is critical to preventing its progression. Such 'self-monitoring' allows for intervention to occur. Consequently, several measures can be taken to assist the client in modifying the 'nurturer' pattern. For example, helpees can be focused upon the particular ideologies they maintain — 'I'm unable'; 'Take care of me' — as well as their strong need for dependence. In conjunction, their fear (and frequently abject terror) may call for direct attention and necessitate considerable ego building and supportive strategies (Blanck and Blanck, 1974, 1979; Saul and Warner, 1975) on the counselor's part. Also, along with these efforts, the future implications of the client's current behaviors seemingly merit exploration; following this, alternative behaviors and options may then be given continued emphasis and accent. Thus, through the counselor's use of such avenues and some of their variants and offshoots, the counselee's awareness of this transference pattern can be facilitated and, perhaps, some modifications evoked.

Counselor as Frustrator
In some cases, clients who enter counseling regard others as frustrators of their experience. When such a transference set is maintained, it is likely

to be expressed explicitly in the therapeutic process. The client evidences a general defensive attitude toward the counselor, as well as a marked cautiousness in sharing and revealing aspects of self. A demeanor of guardedness, suspicion, and distrust typically predominates. The expectation of being frustrated or 'screwed over' often is blatantly apparent, and the counselor can be regarded as fitting into the same mold. This sometimes results in what could be termed the *enter-exit phenomenon*, where the counselee desires to enter into the counseling enterprise but, fearing disappointment, then makes distancing maneuvers. These maneuvers can involve, for instance, the missing of appointments, consistent latenesses, or even the blocking or depletion of associations (Kris, 1982). In such situations a test of the counselor is being made, and the therapist's response to the test can have a significant impact on both the process and outcome of counseling.

The counselor's recognition of this transference pattern can come through various channels. Initially, however, there may be a general feeling of uneasiness and tension in being with the client. The helper can feel on edge and lightly tiptoe about the counselee, as if walking on eggshells. Such an uneasiness results in a careful, ever-vigilant monitoring of responses and actions. As these aspects progress, the helper can withdraw increasingly in the counseling situation, thus becoming more and more unavailable for the client. Where counselors do not recognize their continuing unavailability, they are likely to experience further, more deleterious affects in the counseling relationship, such as an intense dislike for the client, hostility, and even a countertransference hate reaction (Winnicott, 1949).

To prevent the occurrence of such a marked deterioration in therapy, the counselor must closely attend to personal experience and use this to better understand and be more prepared for managing the transference. In such situations, the client often needs to rework early experience via the counselor. That is, the therapeutic atmosphere becomes a place in which the issue of basic trust versus mistrust (Erikson, 1963, 1980) is recapitulated; it is hoped that such reworking will result in the client's development and establishment of a different, less distancing set regarding self and others. The counselor's interventions, then, seemingly should focus on considerable relationship and trust-building gestures, including mirroring the client's experiences, empathizing, and clarifications (Basch, 1983; Paul, 1978). As the relationship develops, confrontations that reflect the helpee's 'enter-exit' struggle, along with counselor disclosures regarding the 'walking on eggshells' experience, can be of value in heightening awareness. More basically, the client's expectations of distrust and the purpose of these expectations merit attention. In many such cases, the reconstruction of early life events, even the recapturing of some preverbal manifestations, may occur as counseling proceeds (Anthi, 1983; Blum, 1980; Brenman, 1980; Greenacre, 1981).

Counselor as Nonentity

This transference pattern typically involves a perceptual interactional set in which the client regards the counselor as an inanimate figure devoid of needs, wishes, hopes, and hurts. As such, the counselee is prone to extreme volubility and action in the counseling session. Thought pressure is pronounced, and the client may move quickly and hurriedly from one topic to another. This 'topic shifting' aspect serves a self-stimulating function, with the client infrequently maintaining a focus for any sustained period of time. Consequently, no direction or binding theme seems to emerge from the helpee's communications. Thus, the counseling hour can proceed in a rather aimless, desultory manner if some means of intervention is not advanced.

When subjected to this interactional style, the counselor is apt to feel overwhelmed initially. The barrage of words and topical changes that are often presented in machine gun fashion take the helper aback and the counselor may then react with reserve and subduedness. Such a 'pulling back' allows the therapist the opportunity to evaluate more effectively the situation and, thereby, recoup both perspective and attitude. If this should not occur, however, further and more varied reactions are likely to surface in the helper's experience. These can include feelings of being used and manipulated or of being markedly discounted and unacknowledged. More pronounced manifestations involve a sense of intense uselessness in relation to these counselees, along with considerable feelings of frustration and resentment toward them.

Intervention with such clients can be especially onerous, primarily because they're so adept at controlling and manipulating the conversational flow. Consequently, for any form of relationship contact and mutuality to be established, the counselor must often maintain a firm and persistent manner in the counseling situation. This can involve the repeating of questions, interpretations, and reflections to the client, particularly if these continue to be ignored or go unrecognized over time. More directly, the client's consistent tendency to pass off the helper's comments can be pointed out. Such a move allows both counselor and client conjointly to assess their ongoing interactions and, thereby, may lay the beginning for a more effective, genuine therapeutic relation.

In addition, the counselor can also focus counselees on their verbal push (or verbal diarrhea as it's been termed [Pine, 1981]), as well as their seeming intolerance for or possible fear of quietness and reflection. Although this frequently allows for heightened self-awareness, such awareness can also lead the client to experience feelings of marked depression and emptiness. Where these circumstances arise, the counselor's provision of ego supportive gestures can prove vital. Thus, with the helper's ongoing support and facilitation, the client then has the opportunity to work through unresolved issues and, hopefully, approach a more satisfying and congruent lifestyle.

In having examined this transference style, as well as the ones that have preceded it, there are innumerable ways in which transference phenomena become manifest in counseling. The patterns surveyed here, though not all-inclusive in scope, seemingly indicate some of the immense implications these behaviors have for counseling process and outcome. As such, the issue of transference seems to be of considerable significance in the therapeutic relationship and, thereby, merits both the counselor's attention and scrutiny. It is hoped, then, that this article has heightened readers' sensitivity to the impact of the transference phenomenon. Most importantly, it is hoped that this article will assist counselors in better recognizing and managing clients' transference behaviors.

References

Adatto, C.P. (1977) 'Transference phenomena in initial interviews', *International Journal of Psychoanalytic Psychotherapy*, 6: 3–13.

Anthi, P.R. (1983) 'Reconstruction of preverbal experiences', *Journal of the American Psychoanalytic Association*, 31: 33–58.

Arlow, J.A. (1979) 'Psychoanalysis', in R.J. Corsini (ed.), *Current psychotherapies* (2nd ed.) (pp. 1–43). Itasca, IL: F.E. Peacock.

Basch, M.F. (1980) *Doing psychotherapy*. New York: Basic Books.

Basch, M.F. (1983) 'Empathic understanding: a review of the concept and some theoretical considerations', *Journal of the American Psychoanalytic Association*, 32: 101–26.

Bellak, L. and Faithorn, P. (1981) *Crises and special problems in psychoanalysis and psychotherapy*. New York: Brunner/Mazel.

Blanck, G. (1976) 'Psychoanalytic technique', in B.B. Wolman (ed.), *The therapist's handbook* (pp. 61–86). New York: Van Nostrand Reinhold.

Blanck, G. and Blanck, R. (1974) *Ego psychology: theory and practice*. New York: Columbia University Press.

Blanck, G. and Blanck, R. (1979) *Ego psychology II: psychoanalytic developmental psychology*. New York: Columbia University Press.

Blum, H.P. (1980) 'The value of reconstruction in adult psychoanalysis', *International Journal of Psycho-Analysis* 61: 39–52.

Brenman, E. (1980) 'The value of reconstruction in adult psychoanalysis', *International Journal of Psycho-Analysis*, 61: 53–60.

Colby, K.M. (1951) *A primer for psychotherapists*. New York: The Ronald Press.

Dinkmeyer, D.C., Pew, W.L. and Dinkmeyer, D.C., Jr. (1979) *Adlerian counseling and psychotherapy*. Monterey, CA: Brooks/Cole.

Erikson, E.H. (1963) *Childhood and society* (2nd ed.). New York: W.W. Norton.

Erikson, E.H. (1980) 'On the generational life cycle: an address', *International Journal of Psycho-Analysis*, 61: 213–23.

Fine, R. (1975) *Psychoanalytic psychology*. New York: Jason Aronson.

Friedman, L.J. (1970) *Psychoanalysis: uses and abuses*. New York: Pocket Books.

Gelso, G.J. (1979) 'Gratification: a pivotal point in psychotherapy', *Psychotherapy: Theory, Research and Practice*, 16: 276–81.

Gill, M.M. (1979) 'The analysis of the transference', *Journal of the American Psychoanalytic Association*, 27: 263–88.

Greenacre, P. (1981) 'Reconstruction: its nature and therapeutic value', *Journal of the American Psychoanalytic Association*, 29: 27–46.

Greenson, R.R. (1971) 'The "real" relationship between the patient and the psychoanalyst', in M. Kanzer (ed.), *The unconscious today* (pp. 213–32). New York: International Universities Press.

Greenson, R.R. (1972) 'Beyond transference and interpretation', *International Journal of Psycho-Analysis*, 53: 213–17.

Kernberg, O. (1965) 'Notes on countertransference', *Journal of the American Psychoanalytic Association*, 13: 38–56.

King, P. (1980) 'The life cycle as indicated by the nature of the transference in the psychoanalysis of the middle-aged and elderly', *International Journal of Psycho-Analysis*, 61: 153–60.

Kris, A.O. (1982) *Free association: method and process*. New Haven: Yale University Press.

Langs, R. (1973) *The technique of psychoanalytic psychotherapy* (vol. 1). New York: Jason Aronson.

Langs, R. (1974) *The technique of psychoanalytic psychotherapy* (vol. 2). New York: Jason Aronson.

Langs, R. (1975) 'Therapeutic misalliances', *International Journal of Psychoanalytic Psychotherapy*, 4: 77–105.

Langs, R. (1978) *The therapeutic interaction: a synthesis*. New York: Jason Aronson.

Langs, R. (1980) *Interactions: the realm of transference and countertransference*. New York: Jason Aronson.

Langs, R. (1982) *Psychotherapy: a basic text*. New York: Jason Aronson.

Laughlin, H.P. (1979) *The ego and its defenses* (2nd ed). New York: Jason Aronson.

Leavy, S.A. (1980) *The psychoanalytic dialogue*. New Haven: Yale University Press.

MacKinnon, R.A. and Michels, R. (1971) *The psychiatric interview in clinical practice*. Philadelphia: W.B. Saunders.

Mosak, H.H. (1979) 'Adlerian psychotherapy', in R.J. Corsini (ed.), *Current psychotherapies* (pp. 44–94). (2nd ed.) Itasca, IL: F.E. Peacock.

Nacht, S. (1959) 'Psychoanalytic therapy' in S. Nacht (ed.), *Psychoanalysis of today*. (pp. 78–98). New York: Grune & Stratton.

Neubauer, P.E. (1980) 'The life cycle as indicated by the nature of the transference in the psychoanalysis of children', *International Journal of Psycho-Analysis*, 61: 137–44.

Panken, S. (1981) 'Countertransference reevaluated', *The Psychoanalytic Review*, 68: 24–44.

Paolino, T.J. (1981) *Psychoanalytic psychotherapy: theory, technique, therapeutic relationship and treatability*. New York: Brunner/Mazel.

Paul, I.H. (1978) *The form and technique of psychotherapy*. Chicago, IL: University of Chicago Press.

Pine, F. (1981) 'In the beginning: contributions of a psychoanalytic developmental psychology' *International Review of Psycho-Analysis*, 8: 15–33.

Reid, W.H. (1980) *Basic intensive psychotherapy*. New York: Brunner/Mazel.

Saul, L. and Warner, S. (1975) 'Mobilizing ego strengths', *International Journal of Psychoanalytic Psychotherapy*, 4: 358–86.

Singer, E. (1970) *Key concepts in psychotherapy* (2nd ed.). New York: Basic Books.

Storr, A. (1980) *The art of psychotherapy*. New York: Methuen.

Winnicott, D.W. (1949) 'Hate in the countertransference', *International Journal of Psycho-Analysis*, 30: 69–75.

Winnicott, D.W. (1975) 'Clinical varieties of transference', in D.W. Winnicott, *Through pediatrics to psycho-analysis* (2nd ed.). New York: Basic Books.

Discussion Issues

1 How important is working with transference phenomena in
   your approach to counselling? Why does it have such
   great/moderate/little importance?
2 Think of examples when clients have adopted towards you
   each of the transference patterns listed by Watkins? How did
   you respond and what were the outcomes?
3 Which transference patterns other than those listed by Watkins
   have your clients adopted towards you? How did you respond
   and what were the outcomes?
4 Which transference patterns do you find most difficult to deal
   with in counselling? Why?
5 Do you find that a sizeable number of your clients tend to
   adopt a particular transference pattern towards you? If so
   describe this pattern and speculate why you think this occurs?
   Do you consider, for example, that there is anything about
   you that elicits such a particular pattern from your clients?
   If so, what are the implications of this?

9 Countertransference: Its Impact on the Counseling Situation

C. Edward Watkins, Jr

Overview

The concept of countertransference is discussed. Some typical behaviors and patterns that illustrate countertransference are identified and described.

Countertransference is a concept that has particular relevance for the counselor. Though it may sound foreign and perhaps irrelevant, it draws attention to the counselor's attitudes and behavior and what impact they have on the counseling situation (Klar and Frances, 1984; MacKinnon and Michels, 1971; Storr, 1980). Countertransference is also important because it derives from some type of counselor identification with the client (Beres and Arlow, 1974). The counselor's identification with the client can be positive or negative and can result in the manifestation of constructive or destructive countertransference behaviors. This article will discuss the concept of countertransference. Some definitions of countertransference will be considered, and four types of countertransference patterns will be described. It is hoped that the counselor will be helped in (a) conceptualizing the countertransference concept, (b) identifying some of the manifestations of countertransference, and (c) becoming increasingly aware of the effects of countertransference behaviors in the counseling relationship.

Conceptualizing Countertransference

Before proceeding, it seems necessary to offer some definitions of counter-transference. This term has been defined in several different ways in the literature and, as a result, discussions of it frequently have proven confusing. Such confusion seems to be well-reflected in the following passage from Strupp (1973).

This article is reprinted by kind permission of the American Association for Counseling and Development from the *Journal of Counseling and Development* (1985), 63: 356–9.

> Even today...there is widespread disagreement as to what the term comprises. For example, distinctions have been made between positive and negative countertransference; some writers insist that all feelings of the therapist should be included; others differentiate between whole and partial responses to the patient; still others restrict the term to the therapist's unconscious reactions. (p. 32)

Though this passage was written over 15 years ago, it continues to mirror many of the disagreements that surround countertransference (see Panken, 1981).

Countertransference refers to some of the thoughts, feelings, and behaviors that the counselor experiences in relation to clients. The nature of these thoughts, feelings, and behaviors, however, is a matter of debate. More specifically, in examining the literature, there seem to be two basic approaches to conceptualizing countertransference: the classical and the totalistic (Kernberg, 1965). The former is considered a somewhat restrictive interpretation, in which countertransference is viewed as those distorting elements that the counselor actualizes in the counseling situation. As Reid (1980) stated, 'These are displacements onto the patient of emotional material which in actuality stems from the therapists internal representations of important persons from his (or her) own past' (p. 78). Others have supported or confirmed Reid's statement, defining countertransference as the therapist's (a) uncounscious reactions toward clients (Colby, 1951), (b) apperceptive distortions (Bellak and Faithorn, 1981), and (c) misperceiving and misresponding to counselees as a result of unresolved conflicts (Arlow, 1979). Thus, countertransference is viewed as inappropriate and 'bad'; it is a phenomenon that the counselor must overcome and work against vigorously. The ideal counselor attitude is one of neutrality.

In contrast to the restrictive, classical definition of countertransference is the totalistic approach. This approach considers all of the counselor's thoughts, feelings, and behaviors to be countertransference manifestations. Everything the counselor does or experiences is defined as countertransference. The problems inherent in the totalistic conceptualization are fairly explicit. First, the approach is unduly amorphous; second, it is overly inclusive in scope (Panken, 1981). Should this definitional approach be adopted, the usefulness of the countertransference concept seems diminished. Not only is the term diluted, but it tends to acquire a vague, unspecific, and meaningless quality. It then offers little from a theoretical or practical standpoint.

Though the classical and totalistic viewpoints are dominant in the literature, a third approach to conceptualizing countertransference has been presented within the past decade. This perspective, which has been described and elaborated on by Blanck (1973) and Blanck and Blanck (1979), conceives of countertransference as possessing both positive and negative elements. In other words, countertransference can be for better or worse in counseling and psychotherapy. It can prove destructive, but it too can be a constructive facet in the therapeutic relationship. Such an approach to countertransference seems to provide a more realistic view of the concept than do the classical and totalistic vantages. Blanck and Blanck's perspective incorporates the classical definition and recognizes the impeding aspects of countertransference behaviors. At the same time, their approach does not seem too broad; thereby, amorphousness and overinclusiveness are avoided.

A helpful supplement to the Blancks' work is Weisman's (1973) discussion of types of countertransference. Specifically, Weisman identifies four types of countertransference that can occur in counseling: (a) complementary, (b) antagonistic, (c) parallel, and (d) tangential. Whereas complementary and parallel countertransferences can be facilitative, those of an antagonistic and tangential nature are generally destructive. For a more thorough and detailed explanation of the positive and negative aspects of countertransference, the reader is referred to Blanck (1973) and Blanck and Blanck (1979). Discussions of the classical and totalistic approaches can be found in Kernberg (1965) and Panken (1981). As a further note, some excellent articles on countertransference are provided in Langs's (1981) *Classics in Psychoanalytic Technique*.

In this article the conceptualization of countertransference as a positive and negative force in counseling is recognized and endorsed. Though papers addressing each of these aspects seem needed, this effort will restrict itself to examining those countertransference behaviors that can be impeding, interfering, and destructive to the counseling relationship. Because of the serious effects of such behaviors, their recognition and management by the counselor seem critical.

Identification and Countertransference

Prior to a description of specific kinds of countertransference behaviors, consideration of the 'why' of such patterns may help in clarifying the material to follow. Why does countertransference arise in the counseling situation? To answer this question, the concept of identification must be examined. Identification refers to the counselor's ability to identify or share with clients in their experiences. It is crucial not only to the general practice of counseling, but perhaps is necessary for helpers to work with any client that they assist. When an optimal identification exists, the therapist is able to relate to and understand the client and still maintain an appropriate distance. When there is no optimal identification, the counselor–client relationship tends to be compromised and, consequently, the helper will have difficulty in empathizing with the counselee.

The ways in which identification occurs can be many and varied. In understanding these means, it is important that *identificatory pathways* or *identificatory mechanisms* that inhere in the counseling relationship be recognized and given ample attention. Identificatory pathways are avenues through which identification between counselor and client is fostered or impaired. Some of these avenues include: (a) values (Are the therapist and client similar, very dissimilar, or somewhere in between where values are concerned?); (b) demeanor (How alike or at odds are counselor and client in regard to their attitudes and behavior?); (c) language (Do therapist and counselee share a similar language?); (d) physical appearance (How might discrepancies between the physical appearances of counselor and client create problems in identification?); and (e) expectations (Are the counselor's and client's therapy goals and expectations similar or dissimilar?).

It seems tenable that identificatory pathways are actualized from the first contact between therapist and client. More pointedly, even as counselor and client make their initial greeting, they are closely monitoring and scrutinizing each other. This occurs on both conscious and unconscious levels and is apt to be ongoing throughout the therapy's duration. When the client's evaluations result in positive identifications with the helper, the likelihood of continuing counseling is increased. When assessments prove unduly negative, however, the probability of termination or strain in the therapeutic relationship is enhanced.

Just as the client's evaluations are important, so too are the therapist's assessments of and identification with the client. In considering this aspect, it is helpful to conceptualize counselor identification as existing on a continuum. The midpoint and its surrounding portion can be regarded as the 'area of optimal identification'. At the right extreme of the continuum is overidentification; on the far left is disidentification. Overidentification represents those behaviors of the counselor in which distance is lost. In other words, the therapist becomes overly enmeshed in the client's material and is unable to remain adequately separated from it. Disidentification is quite an opposite phenomenon, involving a failure of the counselor to identify with the client effectively. Generally, disidentification entails a distancing of the therapist from the helpee and frequently includes such counselor behaviors as aloofness, coldness of manner, lack of empathy for the client, antagonism, and hostility.

As a result of the counselor's overidentifications or disidentifications with the client, impeding and interfering countertransference behaviors tend to arise in the counseling situation. Such behaviors arise when 'the client's transference or nontransference reactions touch the counselor in an unresolved area and result in conflictual and irrational internal reactions' (Peabody and Gelso, 1982: 241). Consistent with what can be provoked through the pathways of demeanor, language, and expectations, among others, the content of the client's communications also is of particular and primary importance. The client's sharings affect the therapist in diverse fashion. Some disclosures will prove of neutral impact, whereas others will stimulate positive and pleasant fantasies in the counselor. In contrast, as Peabody and Gelso (1982) indicated, other aspects of the client's material will arouse the helper's own unresolved and conflictual areas. Because circumstances of these types easily give rise to counselor overidentifications or disidentifications, some of the manifestations and effects of these identification problems will be considered subsequently.

Contertransference Behaviors in the Counseling Situation

The forms that countertransference can take are myriad. Drawing upon the preceding discussion, four clusters of behaviors seem particularly prominent: (a) overprotective, (b) benign, (c) rejecting, and (d) hostile. The first two types are examples of overidentification, while the latter two illustrate the disidentification concept.

Overprotective Countertransference
This pattern reveals itself through the counselor's oversolicitous attitude toward clients. The helper primarily regards clients as fragile and infantile, as individuals who are in need of considerable care and protection. As a result, he or she is apt to guard, shield, and insulate them. For instance, when sharing personal observations or hypotheses about the client, the counselor fairly consistently can cushion and pad these unnecessarily. An excessive amount of qualifiers can be used, and disclaimers or apologetic remarks can be made concomitantly (for example, 'I'm wondering if you might possibly be experiencing that because. . . .But you see, that's just an idea or guess and nothing more. It's just a passing thought. That's all'). Not only are such statements cushioned, they are diluted so much that their impact or effect is virtually lost. Clients, then, are discouraged from considering the full implications of the counselor's observations.

Another related form of overprotection occurs when the therapist does not allow clients to experience hurt, anxiety, or guilt. Anxiety, for example, can be calmed or prevented through the counselor's use of soothing, balmy statements. Hurt can be allayed in a similar manner (for example, 'It'll be all right. It'll be fine.'), and guilt can be relieved through rationalizations or urgings that, 'You'll know better next time.' Whatever the case, these moves by the counselor prove to be hampering, because they tend to short-circuit counselees' individual struggles for self-mastery. Clients are not given ample opportunity to grapple with their personal issues and, consequently, resolution of their concerns is not likely to be achieved.

The overprotective pattern resembles the relationship that exists between an overly solicitous parent and his or her child. In the counseling situation, counselor and client can maintain a similar sort of relationship, with the former acting in a parental, protective fashion and the latter behaving in an infantile manner. An interaction of this type can be termed collusive, for both counselor and counselee collude in the perpetuation of an unhealthy and detrimental counseling dialogue. One of the most harmful facets of such a relationship is that of mutual projection. More specifially, just as the client projects blame onto others, so too does the counselor. The helper shares in externalizing the locus of the counselee's problems. Therefore, the client is not aided in recognizing personal involvement in or developing strategies for coping with problematic areas. Instead, the client's problems are believed to be 'their' fault.

In addition to these manifestations, there are other ways in which over-protective behaviors can be actualized. One method is that of talking lower than usual when with the client. It is as if the counselor wants to shield the helpee from loud verbal stimulation. As a consequence, voice pitch may be lowered, normal rate of speech reduced, and a balmy tone of voice used. Another evidence of this pattern also can be seen in particular physical gestures, such as patting the client on the back, hugging, or patting the client's hands. Each of these behaviors can be infantilizing and can thereby futher induce or reinforce dependency in the client.

In concluding the discussion of this pattern, it must be recognized that the manifestations examined so far have related specifically to direct counselor–client interactions. Nevertheless, overprotective behaviors can occur outside the counseling situation. While at home or occupied in leisure pursuits, the counselor can worry excessively about a client. Sometimes such worry can take on an obsessional quality, with the therapist being unable to remain substantially separated from the helpee. Other related behaviors include fantasizing about the counselee, desires for extra-therapeutic contact, and considerable curiosity regarding the client's day-to-day affairs. When these events occur, the deleterious nature of the counseling relationship for both counselor and client can be quite pronounced.

Benign Countertransference

Benign countertransference shares some characteristics with the over-protective pattern; however, it has a number of sufficiently distinctive aspects that seem to merit review. Such a cluster of behaviors frequently emerges when the counselor experiences an intense need to be liked by a particular client. Still another reason can be the therapist's fear of a client's anger (see Haldipur, Dewan and Beal, 1982). The helper is afraid that the counselee, if nettled or caused displeasure of any kind, will become uncontrollably angry. In these situations the primary fear of the counselor tends to be, 'Will I be able to handle the client's anger or will I be overwhelmed by it?'

To guard against the possibility of client rejection or anger, the counselor can create a benign, bland counseling atmosphere. Generally, the milieu between counselor and counselee can be characterized as friendly, cheerful and optimistic. A focus on the positive predominates, and limited consideration is given to the negative or problematic. The defense mechanism of denial often is shared by both therapist and helpee, and concerted, collusive attempts are made to maintain the overly positive nature of the relationship. In essence, it could be said that the counselor strives to perpetuate a sameness in the counseling relationship; thus, exploration of the client's concerns frequently lacks any real depth or incisiveness.

When benign countertransference behaviors emerge, the character of the counselor–client dialogue can take on decidedly distinctive qualities. The counseling relation often moves from a therapeutic stance to one that is peer to peer. That is, counselor and counselee interact as if they were friends or intimates. Should this situation arise, it usually will follow a developmental progression. Initially, therapist and client engage in a great deal of idle chatter. Pleasantries are exchanged and discussion about extraneous events tends to take place excessively. As counselor and client become better acquainted, there is a mutual sharing in the counseling interchange; consequently, both parties talk in equivalent amounts, with the helper relating as much as the helpee. In cases where these circumstances develop, the counselor is apt to be not only overly disclosing, but overly gratifying as well. The danger of such behaviors is that therapeutic distance is lost; therefore, the dialogue between counselor and client degenerates into either a general 'rap session' or merely another friendly exchange.

Rejecting Countertransference

Like the overprotective pattern, rejecting countertransference behaviors often involve a view of clients as dependent and needy. Instead of moving to protect and shield these people, however, the therapist acts in a way that is rather punitive in nature. An attitude of coolness and aloofness is maintained, and moves are made to establish a sense of considerable distance and separateness between counselor and client (see Cutler, 1958). A counselor who acts in this way can be characterized as minimally involved or as remaining continually on the periphery. A real feeling of mutuality and cooperation does not tend to develop in the therapeutic relationship, and the unilateral quality of the counselor–client dyad is markedly prominent.

The dynamics that give rise to this pattern can be many and varied. In some cases, though, it seems as if the counselor is responding unconsciously to one or two basic issues: (a) fear of demands by others, and (b) fear of being saddled with responsibility for someone else's welfare. As a result, the counselor attempts arduously to remain distant. It is best not to let others get too close, for if they did, what would happen? Where these dynamics emerge, the work between counselor and client at best will be of a 'brief therapy' type.

Considering the detrimental effects of the rejecting countertransference, it is important to examine briefly what the counselor does behaviorally vis-à-vis the client. For one, the helper's empathic understanding of the client can be used in an abusive fashion (Szalita, 1981). That is, such understanding can be used against rather than for the counselee. Interpretive statements can be delivered in a pointed, sharp manner that can provoke hurt and further create distance in the counseling dyad. The therapist also may abruptly dispense with the client's solicitations for opinions or input, saying rather coldly and pointedly, 'That's your decision' or 'That's up to you, not me'.

In conjunction with these explicit behaviors, the counselor can engage in several indirect and implicit withholding reactions. There may be a failure to intervene, even when some form of intervention is sorely needed. The counselor, for instance, can allow clients to wallow and flounder unduly in their anxiety. This can be particularly disturbing for counselees who suffer from abandonment fears or have a tenuous grasp on reality. The therapist, by indulging in withdrawing and withholding behaviors, 'hangs the client out to dry.' One way this can happen is through the unnecessary and extensive use of silence. A protracted period of counselor nonresponsiveness tends to heighten both the abandonment fears and anxiety of some clients. For them, the lack of connection via words can stimulate not only a panic state, but also depersonalization and derealization. Thus, the counselor's withholding, whether it be implicit or explicit in presentation, can have a considerable negative impact on the counseling relationship.

Hostile Countertransference

Hostile countertransference behaviors often evolve from two primary sources: (a) the counselor's seeing something (for example, a particular behavior or attitude) in the client that he or she dislikes or detests, and (b) fear of being infected by the counselee's disturbing behavior or pathology. In an attempt to not be like the client, the counselor tends to create distance in the therapeutic relationship. A disidentification is felt between therapist and client, and the therapist attempts to further this disidentification. Hostility can be used to effectively increase the gap. Generally, hostile reactions or behaviors are both overt and covert in their expression.

In manifesting hostile behaviors, counselors can be somewhat verbally abusive to clients. This could involve, for example, being short, curt or blunt when communicating with the helpee. Also, questions can prove particularly bothersome and be met with a rather bluff response. In other cases, where resentments mount and continue to build, the counselor may subtly enjoy it when the client experiences considerable turmoil. The therapist maintains the attitude of 'that's what you deserve' and can become indifferent to some of the client's struggles. Still other evidences of hostile countertransference can be seen in the therapist who consistently is late or misses a certain helpee's appointments. As can be discerned, the ways in which counselor hostility occurs are myriad. For a thorough discussion, refer to Langs (1974).

The therapeutic consequences of hostile behaviors are fairly explicit: strain between counselor and client is anticipated. This can lead to a mutually abusive relationship in which both parties resent and persistently castigate each other. Sometimes such a relationship is maintained because it meets the needs of therapist and client; at other times, a termination by the client takes place. More pernicious, however, is the relationship that involves the counselor as abuser and client as willing recipient of the abuse. A counselor-counselee interaction of this type tends to be sado-masochistic in nature, with the former manifesting sadistic qualities and the latter playing out the role of masochist. The emotional ramifications of this are dire for the client. Counseling works only to reinforce and futher entrench pre-existing structure and behavior patterns. Thus, therapy becomes negative and deteriorative in effect, rather than positive and constructive.

Implications for the Counseling Relationship

Destructive countertransference patterns can have a significant and pervasive effect on the counseling relationship. They can erode any sense of trust or rapport that may have developed between counselor and client. They also can result in a counseling interaction that is unidirectional; that is, when countertransference behaviors become prominent, it frequently happens that counseling serves the needs of the counselor more so than those of the client. The counselor's manifestation of destructive countertransference patterns can take various forms, ranging from the seemingly benevolent to the malevolent. Whatever the type, such patterns generally are negative for the client and have a deteriorative personal impact. Their prevalence may be one reason for the many premature terminations that occur in counseling settings.

Because of the harmful effects, it seems particularly important that the counselor attempt to understand destructive countertransference patterns. In attempting to alleviate or eliminate these patterns, the characteristic of self-awareness seems to be critical. It is the first and foremost characteristic that is needed by and required of the counselor. To develop or refine such awareness, the counselor must be ever attuned to personal thoughts, feelings and behaviors that are experienced in relation to clients. Therefore, some consistent means of self-monitoring is essential. This can facilitate the counselor's awareness of certain areas in the therapeutic relationship that may prove personally problematic. It also can assist the counselor in effectively managing destructive countertransference behaviors.

There are several different methods that the counselor can use to effectively manage destructive countertransference behaviors. Five methods that the counselor can use to combat acting out in the counseling situation are: (a) self-analysis, (b) personal counseling, (c) supervision, (d) genuineness and self-disclosure, and (e) referral (Watkins, 1983). Each of these methods, though originally described in relation to a specific aspect of countertransference, seems to be applicable to the various patterns presented in this article. The reader is referred to Horney (1942), Patterson (1985), Ramsey (1962) and Watkins (1983) for a description and elaboration of these methods.

In closing, it seems important to consider a somewhat puzzling but interesting question about countertransference: What happens when the counselor manifests countertransference behaviors in the counseling situation, but is completely unaware of doing this? Repressive forces do operate in the counselor as well as in the client. In many cases (where counselor and client are not engaged in some type of collusive relationship), the client may point out the countertransference behaviors to the counselor (Watkins, 1985). In other situations, a sensitive colleague or supervisor can be helpful in noticing something within us that does not seem right. Though these sources can be invaluable, it seems equally, if not more, important that the counselor consider using some of the five previously identified methods not only remedially but preventively. If counselors prevent destructive countertransference patterns, the negative counselor behaviors described here will not be acted out towards clients.

References

Arlow, J.A. (1979) 'Psychoanalysis', in R.J. Corsini (ed.), *Current psychotherapies* (2nd ed.). Itasca, IL: F.E. Peacock.

Bellak, L. and Faithorn, P. (1981) *Crises and special problems in psychoanalysis and psychotherapy*. New York: Brunner/Mazel.

Beres, D. and Arlow, J.A. (1974) 'Fantasy and identification in empathy', *Psychiatric Quarterly*, 43: 26–50.

Blanck, G. and Blanck, R. (1979) *Ego psychology II: psychoanalytic developmental psychology*. New York: Columbia University Press.

Blanck, R. (1973) 'Countertransference in treatment of the borderline patient', *Clinical Social Work Journal*, 1: 110–17.

Colby, K.A. (1951) *A primer for psychotherapists*. New York: The Ronald Press.

Cutler, R.L. (1958) 'Countertransference effects in psychotherapy', *Journal of Consulting Psychology*, 22: 349–56.

Haldipur, C.V., Dewan, M. and Beal, M. (1982) 'On fear in the countertransference', *American Journal of Psychotherapy*, 36: 240–7.

Horney, K. (1942) *Self-analysis*. New York: W.W. Norton.

Kernberg, O. (1965) 'Notes on countertransference', *Journal of the American Psychoanalytic Association*, 13: 38–56.

Klar, H. and Frances, A. (1984) 'Countertransference in focal psychotherapy', *Psychotherapy and Psychosomatics*, 41: 38–41.

Langs, R. (1974) *The technique of psychoanalytic psychotherapy* (vol. 2). New York: Jason Aronson.

Langs, R. (ed.) (1981) *Classics in psychoanalytic technique*. New York: Jason Aronson.

MacKinnon, R.A. and Michels, R. (1971) *The psychiatric interview in clinical practice*. Philadelphia: W.B. Saunders.

Panken, S. (1981) 'Countertransference reevaluated', *The Psychoanalytic Review*, 68: 24–44.

Patterson, C.H. (1985) *The therapeutic relationship: foundations for an eclectic psychotherapy*. Monterey, CA: Brooks/Cole.

Peabody, S.A. and Gelso, C.J. (1982) 'Countertransference and empathy: the complex relationship between two divergent concepts in counseling', *Journal of Counseling Psychology*, 29: 240–5.

Ramsey, G.V. (1962) 'The referral task in counseling', *Personnel and Guidance Journal*, 40: 443–7.

Reid, W.H. (1980) *Basic intensive psychotherapy*, New York: Brunner/Mazel.

Storr, A. (1980) *The art of psychotherapy*. New York: Methuen.

Strupp, H.H. (1973) *Psychotherapy: clinical, research, and theoretical issues*. New York: Jason Aronson.

Szalita, A.B. (1981) 'The use and misuse of empathy in psychoanalysis and psychotherapy', *The Psychoanalytic Review*, 68: 3–21.

Watkins, C.E., Jr. (1983) 'Counselor acting out in the counseling situation: an exploratory analysis', *Personnel and Guidance Journal*, 61: 417–23.

Watkins, C.E., Jr. (1985) 'Frame alterations and violations in counseling and psychotherapy', *American Mental Health Counselors Association Journal*, 7: 104–15.

Weisman, A. (1973) 'Confrontation, countertransference, and context', in G. Adler and P.G. Myerson (eds), *Confrontation in psychotherapy*. New York: Science House.

Discussion Issues

1   To what extent do you find the concept of counter-transference useful in your counselling practice? Why do you find it of great/moderate/little use?
2   In Watkins' article the focus is on counter-transference reactions that *interfere* with the counselling process. How have you used your counter-transference reactions that *enhance* the counselling process (e.g. as a means of gaining a better understanding of your clients' effect on others)? Give examples.
3   Which negative counter-transference reactions do you have a tendency to experience in relating to your clients? How do you know you are experiencing such reactions (e.g. by becoming aware of your feelings, monitoring your thoughts, observing your behavior, etc.)?
4   Specify the ways in which engaging in such activities as personal therapy and supervision of your counselling work has helped you to deal constructively with your negative counter-transference reactions to your clients? Which aspects of these activities have not helped you in this respect?
5   Which aspects of your clients (e.g. attitude, interpersonal style, behaviour) tend to 'pull' negative counter-transference reactions from you?

10 Termination of Individual Counseling: Concepts and Strategies

Donald E. Ward

Overview

The termination of individual counseling is often an inadequately handled process. If managed effectively as a significant stage of counseling, however, it can maximize counseling outcome and the likelihood that clients will maintain new learning and behavior after counseling has ended. Three major functions of termination are described and a number of strategies are presented for attaining each function. In addition, suggestions are given for the facilitative management of premature termination.

The termination of counseling is a process that seems to have been inadequately addressed in the literature, in training programs, and therefore most probably in counseling practice. One contributing factor is the strong human tendency to try to avoid issues of loss by not acknowledging or dealing with them, resulting until recently in a lack of adequate models for productively working with such issues. Another reason is that counseling theoreticians and counselor educators have been mostly interested in emphasizing the establishment of facilitative counseling conditions and the application of facilitative–therapeutic techniques and strategies in order to bring about human growth and change. They have therefore been less interested in the process of reducing and eliminating these conditions and techniques and the strong, productive relationship they create.

A related contributing factor has been that the microcounseling model for teaching counseling skills (Ivey and Authier, 1978), which has been used increasingly in counselor education programs since the late 1960s, has not focused on larger issues of case management such as the termination

This chapter is reprinted by kind permission of the American Association for Counseling and Development from the *Journal of Counseling and Development* (1984), 63: 21–5.

of counseling. Rather, microcounseling models have emphasized the training of specific microskills and the development of a repertoire of attending/ relatationship-building skills and influencing/change skills. In fact, several recent textbooks used in counseling techniques classes contain very little or no material concerning the termination of counseling and its importance (Cormier and Cormier, 1979; Egan, 1982; Hackney and Cormier, 1979; Ivey, 1983).

A theoretical rationale on which to base the effective management of counseling termination must begin with the premise that termination is a process or stage, rather than a sudden cessation of activity (Cavanaugh, 1982; Corey, Corey, Callanan and Russell, 1982; Shulman, 1979). Yalom (1975) emphasized the significance of termination when he stated, 'Termination is more than an act signifying the end of therapy; it is an integral part of the process of therapy and, if properly understood and managed, may be an important factor in the instigation of change' (p. 365). Shulman (1979) suggested that as a general rule-of-thumb, termination should constitute one-sixth of the time of the therapeutic process. The crucial importance of an effective termination process in counseling and psychotherapy has been stressed by a growing number of authors (Goodyear, 1981; Maholick and Turner, 1979; McGee, Schuman and Racusen, 1972; Shulman, 1979: Weiner, 1975). In fact if handled in-appropriately, termination 'may not only conclude this experience without effective change for the member or members, but also so adversely affect individuals that they may not seek further help when necessary' (Hansen, Warner and Smith, 1980: 539). For some clients termination has special significance, especially in cases in which growing up, individualism–separation, and dependency–independency issues are paramount.

Several authors have lamented the lack of attention given to termina-tion in the professional literature (Hansen et al., 1980; Maholick and Turner, 1979; McGee et al., 1972). With the notable exception of an excellent section on the management of termination in Wolberg's (1954) classic textbook on the practice of psychotherapy, little systematic attention has been given to the management of termination until the last decade, during which several factors have converged to provide a rationale for the more sophisticated conceptualization and treatment of the termination process. The aging of the American population has resulted in a move-ment from a youth-oriented culture to a stimulation of interest in the adult developmental process. A model viewing human development as moving through stages throughout the life span, with important transitions to be negotiated between stages, has been described in both the professional (Levinson, Darrow, Klein, Levinson and McKee, 1976; Vaillant and McArthur, 1972) and the popular literature (Sheehy, 1976). A related development was the seminal work of Kubler-Ross (1969) describing the stages of the natural human process of dealing with death.

A third major factor has been the rapid development of the field of group work since Lewin's development of the T-group just after World War II and the accompanying increase in the sophistication of understanding of that process during the last decade. The recognition of the importance of the termination process in group work is best illustrated in the work of Tuckman (1965) and Tuckman and Jensen (1977), both of which reviewed the literature on group developmental stages in order to identify a common model of stages most representative of the various models proposed in the literature at the time. Four stages provided the best fit for the models prior to 1965, and they were tentatively labeled forming, storming, norming, and performing. The literature on group development between 1965 and 1977, however, emphasized termination as a separate and important stage of group work in its own right, and Tuckman and Jensen (1977) consequently identified a fifth stage, adjourning. In fact, McGee et al. (1972) described the value of the termination stage in the following statement:

> The total group and the group psychotherapist are frequently reluctant to face such issues in an open, positive, and therapeutic manner. Yet, if adequately understood and worked through, termination becomes the fruit of group psychotherapy and all that has gone before in the group process. (p. 521)

Recent editions of commonly used group counseling and psychotherapy textbooks include extensive discussion of the termination process in group work (Corey, 1981; Hansen et al., 1980; Trotzer, 1977; Yalom, 1975). The cumulative effect of these developments is to provide a firm rationale upon which to base the more effective management of termination in the individual counseling process.

Conceptualizing Termination

Not only does appropriate termination of individual counseling or psychotherapy involve a number of important issues and activities as part of an identifiable stage of treatment, this stage can be viewed as consisting of three primary functions. First is the function of assessing client readiness for the end of counseling and consolidating learning. A second major purpose includes both resolving remaining affective issues and bringing about appropriate closure of the significant and often intense relationship between the client and the counselor. Effective termination also seeks to maximize transfer of learning and to increase the client's self-reliance and confidence in his or her ability to maintain change after counseling has ended. The extent to which each of these three major functions needs to be emphasized depends upon the individual counseling situation and the needs of specific clients.

Termination Themes and Tasks

A number of important themes and tasks representative of the termination process have been identified, primarily in the literature of group work. Addressing and working through a selected number of these themes and tasks, guided by the needs of each client, will bring about an effective termination process. As has been mentioned, Tuckman and Jensen (1977) used the term 'adjourning' to describe a major task of termination. In other extensive reviews of the group developmental stage literature for the purpose of building comprehensive models of group development, Lacoursiere (1980) identified loss, separation, sadness, and grief as major themes representative of the termination stage, and Cohen and Smith (1976) listed closure, sadness, increased self-efficacy and personal power, and the transfer of learning as key issues. Other important themes are essentially variations of those already listed, such as ending, growing up, autonomy, individuation, reviewing, summarizing, consolidating, and saying good-bye. In an article describing a model to guide the application of theories of counseling and psychotherapy to group work. Ward (1982) identified grieving and leaving as the key tasks in the group termination stage.

Management of the Termination Stage

What are some of the important variables that must be handled properly in order to maximize the effectiveness of work on these themes and tasks during the termination stage? There is general agreement that psychotherapy should not be terminated during the session when it is first verbalized (McGee et al., 1972; Shulman, 1979; Weiner, 1975). In addition to preventing impulsive premature termination, such a policy established termination as a formal stage.

Signs of the Approach of Termination

There are a number of behaviors that may signal the onset of the termination stage, other than direct verbal statements of intent by the client. Among those mentioned in the literature are a decrease in the intensity of the work of counseling, lateness, joking, and intellectualizing (Corey et al., 1982); missed appointments, apathy, acting out, regression to earlier and less mature behavior patterns, withdrawal, denial, expression of anger, and mourning (Shulman, 1979); and feelings of separation and loss, dissolution, futility, impotence, dependency, inadequacy, and abandonment (McGee et al., 1972). If the client increasingly engages in some of these behaviors or feelings but does not verbalize a desire for termination, it may be necessary for the counselor to initiate the process. It is in any case necessary for the counselor to guide the appropriate working through of both task and relationship issues of termination. After the subject has been initiated, it is necessary that the counseling process be restructured to focus on issues of the evaluation and assessment of counseling progress and, therefore, on client readiness for termination.

Evaluation of Termination Readiness

Beginning with Freud (1937/1959), a number of authors have discussed the fact that the counseling or therapeutic process never resolves all problems, removes all symptoms, or results in a complete cure (Weiner, 1975; Wolberg, 1954). Susceptibility to the fantasy quest for 'a complete cure' is a characteristic not uncommon among those in the helping professions, many of whom seem to have a strong proclivity toward windmill-tilting. Some propose the use of specific behavioral goals as a remedy for this tendency toward excess. Although such goals are useful as a benchmark against which counseling progress can be measured, a more sophisticated view recognizes the importance of clinical judgment of client readiness to end the treatment process. Variables such as working through the end of the client–counselor relationship, feelings of grief and sorrow, and learning how to handle endings productively are important, but difficult or impossible to objectify or to be anticipated by clients early in the counseling process. Egan's (1982) problem-management model includes the use of the concept of working to bring about partial gains toward idealized goals such as complete remission of symptoms, psychological wellness, or self-actualization as a method of avoiding unrealistically high or narrow expectations.

Maholick and Turner (1979: 588–9) identified seven areas useful for evaluating client readiness to leave counseling, including:

1 Examining whether initial problems or symptoms have been reduced or eliminated.
2 Determining whether the stress that motivated the client to seek counseling has dissipated.
3 Assessing increased coping ability.
4 Assessing increased understanding and valuing of self and others.
5 Determining increased levels of relating to others and of loving and being loved.
6 Examining increased abilities to plan and work productively.
7 Evaluating increases in the capacity to play and enjoy life.

Another important area is the extent to which the client comes to feel confident to continue to live effectively without counseling.

As these areas are assessed, it may be helpful to classify the client's readiness for termination into a six-category taxonomy of termination type revised and adapted from a model for group therapy developed by McGee et al. (1972). The major criteria include both the completeness of work on the task and the resolution of feelings related to counseling and the ending of the facilitative relationship. The four categories in the original model include (a) leaving with complete denial of any feelings of loss, (b) leaving after a flight into health or sudden breaking through defenses, (c) ending after a specific goal has been partially met with a lack of willingness to move further and little awareness of nonreadiness, and (d) separation after announcing a desire to leave and then appropriately working through evaluation and emotional issues with the counselor. In addition, at least two other categories may be useful, that of the very early terminator who leaves before a strong relationship has been established (thus no feelings of loss exist) and the situation in which the client ends the process despite being aware of his or her nonreadiness, often due to factors external to the counseling process.

Sample Termination Strategies

The presentation of sample counseling strategies useful during the termination process will be organized within the three major functions of termination described earlier, those most useful in goal assessment and consolidation of learning, strategies emphasizing affective issues and closure of the relationship between the counselor and the client, and those that focus on the client's expectations and transfer of learning to a life after counseling has ended. Of course, the categories are not mutually exclusive in actual practice, but do provide a useful system for conceptualizing and selecting strategies. Some of the strategies presented were described in several sources (Corey et al., 1982; Maholick and Turner, 1979; Yalom, 1975), and others originated from my background and experience.

Assessment of Goal Completion and Learning
As has been discussed, restructuring the counseling process toward termination often begins with a shift to a goal assessment focus, and Maholick and Turner's (1979) seven assessment areas can be helpful here. Evaluating progress often begins with listing and measuring changes that the client has made. It is especially important that, although this is a mutual process between the client and counselor, the client assume the primary responsibility for this process during termination, because the counselor will not be present to remind the client of significant gains after the counseling ends. The client may also prepare a progress report for presentation and discussion. Identifying the most significant learnings is an extension or refinement of the comprehensive-listing strategy.

In addition to reviewing progress using written notes or recall, a very enlightening approach involves reviewing a counseling session recorded early in counseling. Clients frequently fail to recall their original status realistically and often tend to minimize gains as they begin to feel, think, and behave more effectively. Another strategy uses actual testing to determine whether or not the client can demonstrate the changes that have occurred, either within the counseling session or *in vivo*. The client's awareness of and confidence in his or her counseling gains may also be tested by a 'devil's advocate' procedure in which the client attempts to convince the counselor of his or her readiness to end counseling. Another quite valuable technique is that in which the client gathers feedback from people outside of the counseling situation related to readiness to sever the counseling process. For a number of reasons judicious planning, care, and processing should be exercised with this technique, primarily because external sources are unpredictable and may be unreliable.

Closure of Affective and Relationship Issues
Opening and inviting exploration of the separation issue is a primary strategy for dealing with affective issues surrounding the cessation of counseling and working through the steps in the closure of the important relationship between the client and the counselor. The client can be encouraged to explore feelings that arise during the termination process, especially those of loss, grief, abandonment, and related issues. The counselor needs to emphasize the fact that although it may be easy and somewhat natural to avoid and deny such feelings, they are very important for the successful completion of counseling. Therefore, the client should focus on, express, and even dramatize such feelings during termination. Reporting dreams and fantasies may help the client to identify and work through these feelings.

Using a photo-album strategy in which the client identifies significant emotional moments that occurred throughout the counseling process by describing imaginary 'snapshots' of those moments and feelings that accompanied them can also bring affective issues into focus. A major strategy in this area is that of immediacy, or increasing the direct discussion of the client and counselor's feelings toward one another and toward the relationship itself. More than any other single indicator, the presence or absence of this increased attention to and working through of relationship factors discriminates between approaches that use the termination process most effectively as a facilitative or therapeutic mechanism in its own right and those that do not. The goal of this emphasis is to lead toward the expression of an appropriate and meaningful good-bye at the actual conclusion of counseling. Clients may summarize their personal reactions to counseling and to the counselor and may give feedback to the counselor concerning what they found facilitative and non-facilitative in the process. As the affective and relationship factors are explored and worked through, some clients may find the idea of developing and signing a 'separation-of-counseling decree' a valuable symbolic statement.

In a special *Personnel and Guidance Journal* issue on dealing with loss and grief, Goodyear (1981) indicated that counselors and therapists should not overlook but should work through their own feelings about the ending of counseling relationships. This is especially true due to the high investment of energy and of self in our work with many clients. There is also the paradox that we continually end those relationships with clients at the point when they have improved their functioning to the extent that they are much more attractive interpersonally and, thus, a continued relationship might be more personally enjoyable to the counselor. The essential guideline in the counselor's resolution of affective and relationship factors during termination is that counselor disclosure during counseling never be detrimental to the client. In other words, where the counselor's use of immediacy benefits the client, it is appropriate to include during counseling sessions, but feelings or issues that would not benefit the client should be worked through outside of the sessions. Genuineness and transparency must be tempered by therapeutic judgment concerning the best interests of the client.

Preparation for Postcounseling Self-reliance
and Transfer of Learning
The third category of termination strategies to be presented are those directed toward the client's expectations for and transfer of learning to life after counseling has ended. One general strategy is to help the client to be specific about at least some expectations and plans. Renewed goal-setting can assist the client in generalizing the goal-setting procedures used in counseling to outside life and to integrating them as a continuing life skill. The client may wish to make self-contracts concerning behavior after counseling has ceased. Rehearsing new roles may also be included at this time. Learning not to diminish, discount, or forget new learning, skills, and the effects of counseling is also a useful strategy.

Although the use of imagery may be effective at any stage of counseling and may be included in any of the three categories of termination strategies, it is also especially valuable in helping the client to anticipate and plan life without counseling. Projecting the future using imagery can be applied in a number of ways, such as imagining oneself applying new learning in a variety of situations and imagining how life will be in 1 month, 6 months, 1 year, and at any point in the client's future. A specific adaptation of this strategy is for the client to imagine how it will feel during the time period when counseling had been scheduled while not going to the session. The client may even plan activities in which to engage at those times. If clients remain anxious or unsure about their readiness to function without counseling, but the counselor judges that most of the work of counseling and termination is complete and the major dependency issues have been resolved, direct systematic desensitization procedures may be used. Desensitization may be combined with cognitive practice, success imagery, and suggestions to maximize the client's expectations for successful functioning and self-reliance following counseling. Another important strategy for preparing the client to leave counseling is counselor feedback including an assessment of the level of client functioning and of issues that the client might anticipate later.

As the termination process continues, increasing the amount of time between sessions is an excellent way of working toward life without counseling. In addition, a number of authors (Corey et al., 1982; Maholick and Turner, 1979; Wolberg, 1954) stress the importance of follow-up letters as long as 5 years after the end of therapy. There are, then, many strategies that can be effective during the termination process. One cardinal rule concerning client readiness for the end of counseling should be emphasized. If, after a number of termination strategies have been applied and other signs of counseling completion are positive, the client remains uncertain about his or her ability to maintain counseling gains without counseling support, then ending the counseling process is inappropriate. Reassessment should be conducted to determine whether the lack of readiness stems from unfinished task work, lingering dependency feelings or incomplete closure of affective issues relating to saying farewell, or incomplete preparation for self-reliance without counseling, after which a recycling of work in the unfinished areas may be undertaken.

Handling Termination when Counseling is Unfinished

Thus far, discussion has emphasized the somewhat ideal situation in which counseling has progressed to the point that most goals seem to have been met and the client willingly cooperates in the meaningful working through of termination issues. Some attention has even been directed at cases in which the client resists or feels unready to end the counseling process. But a major challenge in termination remains to be discussed, that of clients who wish to end counseling before it seems that they are ready.

What Constitutes 'Premature Termination'

Of course, readiness is a subjective concept. Strategies of the evaluation of readiness have been presented. In some cases the client and counselor may agree that counseling is unfinished and that significant problems remain. There are also those cases in which the client believes or purports to believe that the process is complete, despite the counselor's judgment and concern that it is not. Actually, these types of situations account for five of the six types of termination described by McGee et al. (1972) and myself earlier in this article.

Recent studies have attempted to identify the variables responsible for early terminators from university counseling centers, defined as those who do not return for a second or third interview after the intake session. The results, however, have been unclear and somewhat contradictory (Epperson, Bushway and Warman, 1983; Rodolfa, Rapaport and Lee, 1983). On the other hand, Rosenzweig and Folman (1974) identified level of education and several therapist judgment variables as significant predictors of dropouts who completed less than 16 group therapy sessions of an outpatient VA service. Clearly, then, early separation from counseling cannot be neatly defined by the number of interviews completed. Readiness must be judged in terms of the extent to which client problems and ineffective functioning remain, the degree to which these factors negatively affect the client's life and that of significant others, the extent to which the client can be expected to maintain counseling gains on his or her own, and how appropriately the client has been able to work through affective issues surrounding the termination of counseling and of the relationship with the counselor.

Extending Abrupt Endings into a Stage
Yalom (1975) made the important point that premature termination in group therapy is a necessary safety valve due to our imperfect understanding of member selection procedures. One of the problems with nonvoluntary counseling is that this safety valve can no longer operate as easily. This same protective device also serves a useful purpose in voluntary individual counseling, because our treatment methods and matching of treatment and counselor with client are less than perfect. But there still remains the issue of providing the best possible treatment for the client, and this requires some extension of the counseling process beyond the time when the client decides to end it. When the client's ending of counseling is characterized by suddenness, unexpectedness, untimeliness, irrationality, superficiality, or unfavorable reactions from the counselor (McGee et al., 1972), it is critical that the counselor try to extend counseling and restructure the work to include a termination stage. The major purposes of this extended work are to help clients to resolve any negative feelings resulting from counseling itself, to invite clients to continue counseling if they wish, and to work toward an appropriate referral to another counselor or type of treatment or toward increasing the likelihood that the client will reengage in some type of counseling or facilitative experience at a later date.

Ohlsen (1979) and Hansen et al. (1980) suggested that in group work, if the client indicates or the counselor suspects that the client may abruptly sever the counseling process before it is completed, the subject of termination should be openly discussed. If as is the case with some clients, the client simply does not return for a scheduled appointment and does not contact the counselor or agency to reschedule, efforts should be made to contact the client. Some clients may be testing the counselor's concern, may have reached a difficult point in the counseling process, or may be so overwhelmed that they do not believe themselves capable of continuing, and a contact may be all that is needed for productive counseling to resume. Others may very definitely have negative feelings and be resistant to continued counseling. It is suggested that a receptionist phone a client three or four days after the missed appointment to reschedule. If the receptionist is unable to make contact or meets resistance, the counselor can then contact the client and, if the client wishes to end counseling, invite and strongly encourage the client to return for at least one more session to work through any lingering issues, to decide about possible referral, and to help the counselor to understand better the reasons for termination. If these procedures are unsuccessful, a follow-up letter to invite the client to return at any time can be effective. Although less preferable than working with the client in person, it is even possible to work on some of these issues during a telephone call in cases where the client refuses to return or to give the client the name of a referral source in a letter.

Working Through Negative Reactions
It is very important that the counselor help the client who wishes to end the counseling process with significant work remaining to deal with negative reactions and feelings. If the client is willing to engage in an exit interview, there are at least four posssible positive client outcomes that may result: (a) reduction of as many negative influences as possible before the client resumes life without counseling, (b) resolution of critical issues to the extent that the client is able to continue counseling with the same counselor, (c) preparation of the client for gaining maximum benefit from referral to another 'helper,' and (d) increased likelihood that the client will reenter counseling or some other personal growth experience at some future date.

As Yalom (1975) stated when discussing group therapy drop-outs, 'it is up to the therapist to make the experience as constructive as possible, such patients ordinarily are considerably demoralized and tend to view the group experience as "one more failure"' (p. 367). In individual counseling, the same reaction often applies, although the strong feelings may also be directed at the counselor, the agency, or counseling in general. Although clients should be given feedback to assist them in their futures, the extent to which a specific client is confronted with unrecognized, unresolved, and potentially threatening material should be carefully considered in light of whether or not he or she is likely to accept a referral or reenter counseling in the near future (Yalom, 1975). Although some judicious leverage may be carefully applied, frightening the client into further therapy is a questionable policy at best.

The extent to which the client's negative reactions toward the counselor should be resolved also depends on the likelihood of the client accepting a referral and the extent to which such resolution is likely to assist in the continuing counseling process. It took some time in my own counseling practice before I realized that although some referral clients were justifiably upset by their previous treatment, others had been purposely allowed to maintain their negative or ambivalent attitudes toward the previous counselor in order to increase the effectiveness of counseling after the referral. Although it is difficult for counselors to end counseling while unappreciated and unliked by clients, it is sometimes in the client's best interest.

Conclusion

It is possible for the termination of counseling to be handled more effectively today, primarily as a result of knowledge stimulated by the work of Kubler-Ross on death, dying, and the grieving process and by advances in the management of termination in group work. Assessment procedures are available for evaluating client readiness for termination of counseling. Strategies are also available for working through issues of identifying and consolidating gains, resolving affective issues and ending the relationship with the counselor appropriately, and preparing the client to maintain counseling gains after counseling ends. In addition, handling client attempts to leave counseling prematurely in the best interests of the client is a sensitive and important issue.

The guiding principle in the productive management of counseling termination is to treat the termination process as a stage in its own right and therefore to give significant termination issues the attention they deserve. Effective closure of the counseling process in a well-managed termination stage can help to solidify clients' learning and to maximize their continued self-efficacy and success after counseling. The role of effective termination procedures in helping the client to take appropriate and mature leave of the counseling process has been clearly described by Maholick and Turner (1979): 'Termination of therapy can be thought of as a recapitulation of the multiple preceding goodbyes of living. At the same time it is a preparation for being able to deal more adequately and openly with future goodbyes' (p. 584). Or, to paraphrase the bard, 'parting can be such productive sorrow.'

References

Cavanaugh, M.E. (1982) *The counseling experience: a theoretical and practical approach.* Monterey, CA: Brooks/Cole.

Cohen, A.M. and Smith, R.D. (1976) *The critical incident in growth groups: theory and technique.* La Jolla, CA: University Associates.

Corey, G. (1981) *Theory and practice of group counseling.* Monterey, CA: Brooks/Cole.

Corey, G., Corey, M.S., Callanan, P.J. and Russell, J.M. (1982) *Group techniques.* Monterey, CA: Brooks/Cole.

Cormier, W.H. and Cormier, L.S. (1979) *Interviewing strategies for helpers: a guide to assessment, treatment, and evaluation.* Monterey, CA: Brooks/Cole.

Egan, G. (1982) *The skilled helper: models, skills and methods for effective helping* (2nd ed.). Monterey, CA: Brooks/Cole.

Epperson, D.L., Bushway, D.J. and Warman, R.E. (1983) 'Client self-termination after one counseling session: effects of problem recognition, counselor gender, and counselor experience', *Journal of Counseling Psychology*, 30: 307–15.

Freud, S. (1959) 'Analysis terminable and interminable', in J. Strachey (ed.), *Collected papers* (vol. V, pp. 316–57). New York: Basic Books. (Original work published 1937.)

Goodyear, R.K. (1981) 'Termination as a loss experience for the counselor', *Personnel and Guidance Journal*, 59: 347–50.

Hackney, H. and Cormier, L.S. (1979) *Counseling strategies and objectives* (2nd ed.). Englewood Cliffs, NJ: Prentice-Hall.

Hansen, J.C., Warner, R.W. and Smith, E.J. (1980) *Group counseling: theory and process* (2nd ed.). Chicago: Rand McNally.

Ivey, A. (1983) *Intentional interviewing and counseling*. Monterey, CA: Brooks/Cole.

Ivey, A. and Authier, J. (1978) *Microcounseling: innovations in interviewing, counseling, psychotherapy, and psychoeducation* (2nd ed.). Springfield, IL: Charles C. Thomas.

Kubler-Ross, E. (1969) *On death and dying*. New York: Macmillan.

Lacoursiere, R.B. (1980) *The life of groups: group developmental stage theory*. New York: Human Sciences Press.

Levinson, D., Darrow, C.M., Klein, E.B., Levinson, M.H. and McKee, B. (1976) 'Periods in the adult development of men: ages 18–45', *The Counseling Psychologist*, 6(1): 10–15.

Maholick, L.T. and Turner, D.W. (1979) 'Termination: that difficult farewell', *American Journal of Psychotherapy*, 33: 583–91.

McGee, T.F., Schuman, B.N. and Racusen, F. (1972) 'Termination in group psychotherapy', *American Journal of Psychotherapy*, 26: 521–32.

Ohlsen, M.M. (1979) 'Termination techniques with couples groups', *Journal for Specialists in Group Work*, 4: 110–12.

Rodolfa, E.R., Rapaport, R. and Lee, V.E. (1983) 'Variables related to premature terminations in a university counseling service', *Journal of Counseling Psychology*, 30: 87–90.

Rosenzweig, S.P. and Folman, R. (1974) 'Patient and therapist variables affecting premature termination in group psychotherapy', *Psychotherapy: Theory, Research, and Practice*, 11: 76–9.

Shulman, L. (1979) *The skills of helping individuals and groups*. Itasca, IL: Peacock.

Sheehy, G. (1976) *Passages: predictable crises of adult life*. New York: Bantam.

Trotzer, J.P. (1977) *The counselor and the group*. Monterey, CA: Brooks/Cole.

Tuckman, B.W. (1965) 'Developmental sequence in small groups', *Psychological Bulletin*, 63: 384–99.

Tuckman, B.W. and Jensen, M.A.C. (1977) 'Stages of small-group development revisited', *Group and Organization Studies*, 2: 419–27.

Vaillant, G.E. and McArthur, C.C. (1972) 'Natural history of male psychologic health: the adult life cycle from 18–50', *Seminars in Psychiatry*, 4: 415–27.

Ward, D.E. (1982) 'A model for the more effective use of theory in group work', *Journal for Specialists in Group Work*, 7: 224–30.

Weiner, I.B. (1975) *Principles of psychotherapy*. New York: John Wiley.

Wolberg, L.R. (1954) *The technique of psychotherapy*. New York: Grune and Stratton.

Yalom, I.D. (1975) *The theory and practice of group psychotherapy* (2nd ed.). New York: Basic Books.

Discussion Issues

1 How do you judge when your client is approaching readiness to terminate counselling?
2 Under what conditions might you (a) increase the interval between sessions as a way of initiating termination with a client; (b) set a specific date to terminate without first increasing the interval between sessions?
3 How do you deal with the issue of dependency in clients who otherwise appear ready to terminate?
4 What range of feelings do you experience during the termination process? What have you learned about yourself from such experiences?
5 How do you respond when clients wish to terminate counselling prematurely?

Index

Index compiled by Peva Keane

Notes on Contributors

Robert W. Day is an Assistant Professor in Human Development Counseling and Coordination at George Peabody College for Teachers, Vanderbilt University, Nashville.

Margaret L. Fong is an Associate Professor of Counseling at the University of Florida where she is Coordinator of the Mental Health Counseling Programs. She has also been on the faculties of Boston University and the University of Hawaii. Dr Fong has provided consultation and training throughout the United States, in South Asia, and Europe. She has served on the editorial review boards of *Counselor Education and Supervision* and *Western Journal of Nursing Research* and is the author of over fifteen book chapters and journal articles in the field of counseling

Barbara Gresbach Cox was a student in Counselor Education at the time the chapter was written. She is currently operating a private business in Gainesville, Florida.

David E. Hutchins is Associate Professor of Counselor Education at Virginia Polytechnic and State University in Blacksburg, Virginia. He is the developer of the Thinking, Feeling, Acting (TFA) System, a metatheoretical system for integrating cognitive, affective, and behavioral approaches to counseling and psychotherapy. Dr Hutchins is Chair of the Board of Professional Counselors which licenses counselors and therapists in Virginia, and is the author of several books and journal articles.

Robert Manthei is a Senior Lecturer in Education at the University of Canterbury, Christchurch, and coordinator of the Department's Counsellor training programme.

David Matthews is an experienced school counsellor and currently Inspector of Secondary Schools responsible for guidance, counselling and special education.

Robert T. Sparacio is a counseling psychologist intern at Texas A&M University, College Station.

Carole Sutton is a Senior Lecturer in Psychology at Leicester Polytechnic, where she contributes to the education and training of social workers. She is a qualified social worker and worked as such in the fields of health and mental health before studying psychology and joining the Polytechnic.

Terence J. Tracey received his PhD from the University of Maryland in 1981, and is currently an Associate Professor and Chair of the Counseling Psychology Division in the Department of Educational Psychology at the University of Illinois at Urbana-Champaign. He has published numerous studies on the counseling/psychotherapy process and on how clients and therapists influence each other. He has also conducted research in the training and supervision of counselors and therapists.

Donald E. Ward is Professor and Chair of the Counseling Committee at Pittsburg State University, Pittsburg, Kansas. Dr Ward has chaired several national committees in the Association for Specialists in Group Work and has been president of the Kansas Association for

Counseling and Development. He serves on the editorial board of the *Journal for Counseling and Development* and has published a number of articles in professional journals. He is a National Certified Counselor, a Registered Professional Counselor in Kansas, and both a Clinical Member and Approved Supervisor of the American Association for Marriage and Family Therapy.

C. Edward Watkins, Jr received his PhD in counseling psychology from the University of Tennessee at Knoxville in 1984. Previously at North Texas State University, he is currently an Assistant Professor of Counseling Psychology at Kent State University. He is also affiliated with the Northeastern Ohio Universities College of Medicine. His primary research interests include professional issues in counseling psychology, psychological assessment, and psychodynamic counseling.